Innovations in Foreign Language Teaching and Learning in Chinese Higher Education

Qu Lili

  AMERICAN ACADEMIC PRESS

AMERICAN ACADEMIC PRESS

Published in the United States of America

By AMERICAN ACADEMIC PRESS

201 Main Street

Salt Lake City

UT 84111 USA

Email manu@AcademicPress.us

Visit us at http://www.AcademicPress.us

Copyright © 2024 by AMERICAN ACADEMIC PRESS

All rights reserved, including those of translation into foreign languages.

No part of this publication may be reproduced, stored in a retrieval system, or transmitted in any form or by any means, electronic, mechanical, photocopying, recording, or otherwise, now known or hereafter invented, without the prior written permission of the AMERICAN ACADEMIC PRESS, or as expressly permitted by law, or under terms agreed with the appropriate reprographics rights organization. Enquiries concerning reproduction outside the scope of the above should be sent to the Rights Department, American Academic Press, at the address above.

The scanning, uploading, and distribution of this book via the Internet or via any other means without the permission of the publisher is illegal and punishable by law. Please purchase only authorized editions and do not participate in or encourage electronic piracy of copyrighted materials. Your support of the publisher's right is appreciated.

ISBN: 979-8-3370-8909-6

Word count: 134,733

Distributed to the trade by National Book Network Suite 200, 4501 Forbes Boulevard, Lanham, MD 20706

10 9 8 7 6 5 4 3 2 1

Manufactured in the United States of America

Contents

Chapter One Introduction 1

Chapter Two Innovations in Foreign Language Teaching and Learning Theories 10

    2.1 Review of Second Language Acquisition Theories 10
    2.2 Innovation of the Xu-argument 14
    2.3 Innovation of the Production-Oriented Approach (POA) 26
        2.3.1 Construction of POA 26
        2.3.2 Design of POA activities 35
        2.3.3 Research on POA 40
        2.3.4 Critique of POA 45

Chapter Three Innovation in Content of Foreign Language Learning and Teaching 48

    3.1 Review of Content-Based Instruction (CBI) 48
    3.2 Review of Content and Language Integrated Learning (CLIL) 55
    3.3 Innovation in Content and Language Integration (CLI) 57

Chapter Four Innovation in Multimodal Foreign Language Teaching 69

    4.1 Review of multimodal pedagogy 69
    4.2 Innovation in multimodal foreign language teaching in China 74

Chapter Five Innovation in Technology-enhanced Foreign Language Teaching 90

5.1 Review of computer assisted language learning (CALL) 90
5.2 Technology-enhanced language teaching in China 93
    5.2.1 Reform of English teaching: Integration of technologies 93
    5.2.2 Internet-based foreign language teaching research 96
    5.2.3 Research on technology-enhanced foreign language teaching 101
5.3 Technology-enhanced teaching modes 106
5.4 Artificial intelligence and foreign language teaching 118
5.5 Corpus-based language teaching and learning 122

Chapter Six Innovation in Project-Based Language Learning 128

6.1 Review of project-based language learning 128
6.2 Localization of PBLL in China 133

References 141

Chapter One Introduction

Since the reform and opening up more than 40 years ago, foreign language teaching and learning in China's higher education has undergone revolutionary changes. Initially, foreign language education focused on the cultivation of language skills to meet the demand for China's participation in the global economy, and foreign language graduates needed to be proficient in a second language, particularly English listening, speaking, reading, writing, and translation. However, the development of society and economy requires additional skills of foreign language majors. In the new century, the cultivation of interdisciplinary and innovative talents has been more important than ever before. Foreign language learners not only need proficient foreign language skills, but also need to improve their multiliteracies, critical thinking ability, cooperative ability, and innovative ability. In addition, foreign language teaching and learning tends to integrate subject knowledge and information technology, which not only promotes language teaching effectiveness but also enhances learners' abilities in the above-mentioned aspects. To this end, Chinese scholars and researchers of foreign language education actively absorb foreign second language acquisition and foreign language teaching theories, and continuously innovate in theories, methods, and practices according to local conditions, so as to solve the problems and challenges confronting foreign language teaching in the new era. This book mainly introduces the work done by Chinese scholars and researchers in promoting innovations in foreign language teaching in the last 20 years.

In Chapter 2, innovations in foreign language

teaching and learning theories are introduced. Two innovative theories, namely Xu-argument and Production-Oriented Approach are elaborated. Xu-argument proposed by Wang Chuming can be considered a new approach to second language acquisition, which contends that language is acquired through continuation. Xu-argument based tasks require the learner to use his or her imagination to complete, extend and create based on the given discourse. The interaction involved in the tasks maximizes alignment, which brings about approximation between comprehension and production, thus contributing to language acquisition. The other theory, Production-Oriented Approach (POA), was proposed by Wen Qiufang as a teaching theory to address the weaknesses in foreign language instruction in Chinese higher education. POA stresses the role of output in language acquisition, initially basing its construction on Swain's output hypothesis, but uses the term "production" to include not only speaking and writing, but also translating and interpreting. In addition, POA emphasizes both producing and product. POA doesn't adopt the widely held assumption that learning begins with input followed by output, but holds that learning should start with productive activities and end with productive activities. Teaching based on POA consists of three phases: motivating, enabling and assessing, and the designing of corresponding teaching activities is elaborated in the chapter.

Chapter Three presents innovations in teaching content of foreign language instruction. Teaching content cannot be separated from teaching philosophy. Two major teaching approaches concerning what to teach are introduced, namely Content-Based Instruction (CBI) and Content and Language Integrated Learning (CLIL). Despite arguable differences regarding the teaching aim and teaching method, both approaches emphasize the integration of subject matter knowledge into language teaching, and have been acknowledged by researchers and practitioners of tertiary-level foreign language instruction in China. Based on the related concept of CBI and CLIL and taking into consideration of status quo of foreign language teaching in the Chinese context, Chang Junyue proposed a localized approach called Content and Language Integration (CLI). CLI is claimed to expand the curriculum to incorporate systematic disciplinary knowledge so English-major students can receive adequate education to become well-rounded individuals. This approach echoes the call for the cultivation of "New Liberal Arts" talents to meet the higher quality development requirements of China.

Chapter Four introduces innovation in multimodal foreign language teaching in Chinese higher education. There has been a growing interest in the pedagogical application of multimodal research in the field of SLA. A multimodal pedagogy aims to cultivate multiliteracies in language learners so that they can exploit semiotic modes to understand and produce the target language more effectively. With increasing influence of modern media technology, Chinese higher education has seen more research on multimodal foreign language teaching. Zhang Delu has pioneered both theoretical and practical research in this field. He developed a framework for multimodal discourse analysis and research to facilitate the choice of effective practice in foreign language teaching. Zhang also explored "design" in in the selection of modalities in foreign language classroom teaching and proposed the possible stages and methods of teaching as well as principles of selecting appropriate mode systems based on design. In addition, Zhang discussed in depth what multiliteracies are and how to develop them in foreign language learners in the Chinese context.

Chapter Five presents innovations in technology-enhanced foreign language teaching in China. The chapter first reviews four developmental stages of computer-assisted language learning (CALL), and points out that the current stage is ecological CALL. Chinese scholar Chen Jianlin carried out investigations of ecological CALL in English teaching in Chinese higher education as a response to the call for English course reforms by the Ministry of Education. He argues that the assisting role of technology will not transform the old system of foreign language teaching and the comprehensive integration of technologies into foreign language courses is imperative. Following his lead, other researchers probe into theoretical construction and pedagogical practice of integrating technologies into foreign language teaching. For example, a comprehensive framework was constructed to promote the research on Internet-based foreign language teaching that incorporated teaching theory research, teaching factor research and teaching design research.

Chapter Six reviews innovations in project-based language learning (PBLL) in China. PBLL is regarded as a pedagogical strategy in second language acquisition that encourages students' participation and collaboration in order to develop their linguistic and non-linguistic skills. It has been proven that PBLL enhances students' motivation and creativity, and has received generally positive responses from students and teachers. Thus, PBLL has gained popularity in EFL countries, including China. Zhang Wenzhong explored PBLL in the Chinese context, and came up with a localized model through long-term pedagogical practice. The student-centered and creativity-oriented PBLL model features six progression stages promoting integrated comprehensive training. Other Chinese scholars are also actively involved in PBLL research and have identified opportunities and challenges of applying this teaching approach in the Chinese context.

All in all, the innovations discussed in this book are enlightening to future research in the area of foreign language teaching and learning in China. The reviewed previous research demonstrates how Chinese researchers have critically adopted foreign theories and renovated them with their own practical experience in the local context. It's hopeful that the innovative theories and practices will contribute to more effective teaching and learning of foreign languages in China.

Chapter Two Innovations in Foreign Language Teaching and Learning Theories

2.1 Review of Second Language Acquisition Theories

Different theories and views on second language acquisition have sprouted since the second half of the last century and subsequently have had a huge impact on language teaching.

The focus of this section will be on theories that have directly affected foreign language teaching and learning.

SLA theories have long been cognitivist in nature, focusing on the cognitive processes in L2 development. According to Krashen's Monitor Theory (1982), there is a difference between "acquisition" and "learning". L2 acquisition is described as a process similar to L1 acquisition where the learner focuses on meanings of messages while L2 learning is a process where the learner's attention is directed to the forms of the language. Krashen argued that spontaneous speech occurs as a result of acquisition rather than learning, suggesting the importance of focusing on meaning. His "comprehensible input hypothesis" also reflects the view that meaningful and varied linguistic input is essential for developing L2 competence. The pedagogical implication of the hypothesis is that the learner should be exposed to input that is slightly more complex than what the learner has already acquired.

Some theorists believe that language learning primarily takes place through social interaction, where interlocutors adjust their speech to make it more comprehensible to learners. When L2 learners interact, they often use various interactive adjustments to negotiate meaning. The typical adjustments include modifications and simplifications at phonological, lexical, syntaxic or discoursal levels. According to Long's interaction hypothesis (1985), comprehensible input is essential for interlanguage development, but it is interactional adjustments that improve comprehension. Moreover, interaction can include negative feedback necessary for L2 learners to attain higher levels of performance (Long, 1996).

Different from the dominant cognitivist SLA theories, the sociocognitive approach to second language acquisition has a fundamental tenet that L2 development takes place through the mind-body-world activity of which cognitive internationalization of input is only a part. The alignment concept is key to this approach. In L1 interactions, alignment is accounted by the commonality underlying comprehension and production manifested by structural priming or linguistic similarities between language users in production (Pickering and Garrod, 2004). With regard to L2 development, alignment is defined as the means by which human actors dynamically adapt to — that is, flexibly depend on, integrate with, and construct — the ever-changing mind–body–world environments posited by sociocognitive theory (Atkinson et al., 2007). Learning is claimed to be the default process of continually aligning oneself with one's sociocognitive environment, also called dynamic ecological adaptivity. Therefore, alignment is learning in interaction. The sociocognitive approach is presented as a thinking tool for conceptualizing L2 development as a dynamic and interactive process which can be described by trajectories of experience and repertoires of participation.

Recent studies have utilized the notion of

alignment to explore processes of second language acquisition. While alignment studies have primarily focused on L2 interpersonal interactions (Atkinson et al., 2007; Costa et al. 2008), scholars have also attempted to uncover alignment in other forms of interactions. Wang and Wang (2015) coupled comprehension and production in an L2 writing task, which was called a continuation task. In the continuation task, subjects were required to continue in L2 the stories with their endings removed. They found alignment manifested itself in the continuation and concluded that the continuation task could serve as a useful tool for L2 learning.

2.2 Innovation of the Xu-argument

A series of elucidations (Wang, 2016, 2017) on continuation and CEC (completion, extension and creation) leading to language acquisition are referred to as the xu-argument, which is considered a new approach to second language acquisition. To put it simply, language is acquired through continuation. The xu-argument has been developed over a span of twenty-year exploration on efficient and effective foreign language teaching in China (Wang, 2021). It began with "the length approach", which was aimed at solving the problem of low efficiency of English teaching in China. Students were required to write longer compositions to increase output and improve sense of achievement. However, the length approach focused more on writing fluency than accuracy, which was insufficient for improving language use. To provide exemplar for language use, teachers made students continue to write after reading a text with its ending removed (a typical continuation task), which showed surprisingly good effect – longer compositions with less errors. The reasons for the effectiveness of the continuation task hadn't been uncovered until the principle of "learn together and use together" was put forward and researched (Wang, 2009). It can be seen that this principle is evident in the continuation task. The principle puts the factor of context at the heart of language learning. In the continuation task, reading provides the context for language learning immediately followed by language use through writing. Context is useful in comprehending a dialogue or a text, and prompting the learner to activate language that is appropriate for the specific situation. Continuation tasks also require the learner to use his or her imagination to complete, extend and create based on the given discourse. Therefore, context is particularly important for this kind of tasks to be effective.

The xu-argument can be considered an innovation in foreign language learning in China. It builds on earlier SLA theories, such as the interaction theory, and resembles the usage-based theory in that both acknowledge contextual experience and various kinds of interaction. Different from the usage-based theory which connects language acquisition with frequency of exposure, the xu-argument postulates that "learn together and use together" principle underlies second language acquisition. The following concepts explain how the xu-argument can contribute to foreign language teaching and learning. Firstly, continuation links static language knowledge with dynamic content by encouraging creative imitation – imitating language forms in the input for creative production of content. In this way, learning becomes more efficient, and acquisition is more likely to occur. Secondly, continuation serves as the medium between comprehension and production, comprehension always exceeding production. With continuation, production can approximate comprehension further and further. Therefore, two conditions are necessary: incomplete input and an asymmetry between the learner's input and output. Thirdly, continuation makes context play its role to the full in supporting the learner to use appropriate words, structures and style in their work of completion, extension and creation. Fourth, continuation maximizes alignment due to the interaction involved in the task, and alignment brings about approximation between comprehension and production, thus contributing to language acquisition. The more interaction required, the stronger the alignment and the better the learning of language (Wang, 2021).

The xu-argument has enlightened studies involving various continuation tasks to drive learning in interaction, such as integrated reading-writing continuation tasks and integrated reading-translating continuation tasks. The reading and writing integration has been an important form of writing teaching and testing in China, and has been the most researched form of continuation tasks up to now. A number of studies investigate how input affects alignment. First, there are studies on the effects of L1 or L2 input. In Wang and Wang's (2015) study, alignment was found in the reading-writing continuation task performed by the Chinese learners of English who used more lexical items in the original story and committed fewer errors when performing on the English-input task than the Chinese-input task. Similarly, Zhang's (2017) continuation study found that the EFL learners who wrote with English input outperformed those with Chinese input in EFL accuracy and content alignment. Second, there are studies on the linguistic complexity of the input. Peng et al. (2020) investigated how linguistic complexity of the input and its match/mismatch with EFL learner proficiency levels affect performance in reading-writing continuation tasks. It's reported that simplified reading input, when matching the learner proficiency level, resulted in more automatic alignment and greater improvement in accuracy compared to the original more complex input. Yang and Cai (2022) investigated how the linguistic complexity of the input affects L2 writing development in terms of accuracy, fluency, and complexity over a span of 11 weeks. They found that L2 learners could write more accurately with increasingly complex input, and their writing fluency achieved development with constantly simplified input texts. Also, the learners produced more coordinate phrases when receiving input texts with increasing complexity but more dependent clauses when the complexity of input was kept constant. These studies show that linguistic complexity matters for the continuation tasks to facilitate learners' language acquisition.

The different genres of texts in the continuation tasks have different effects on language learning. Zhang and Zhang (2017) investigated the differences in alignment and language errors produced in the continuation writing of narration and argumentation. The findings show that the argumentation writing produces more alignment in words and phrases and fewer language errors than the narration writing. These reviewed studies show that suitable input plays an essential role in enhancing alignment and improving learning effects.

Some other studies explore how to design the continuation task so as to enhance the alignment effect for language learning. To overcome the shortcomings of the continuation task, such as low alignment and low efficiency of learning, Wang et al. (2022) designed the continuation task with cue-induced contextual recurrence and explored its effects on alignment and learning. It is found that the cue significantly increased the length of L2 learners' writings, enhanced their use of the words and phrases in the original context, indicating that the cue can strengthen alignment of the task.

Interaction is the key to the continuation task

in that no interaction means no alignment. To improve interactive alignment between reading and writing, Wang (2018) proposed two variants of the continuation task: the iterative continuation and the comparative continuation. He elaborated the procedures for implementing the two variants in the hope of providing pedagogical guidance for using the continuation task to enhance learning. Subsequently, a series of studies on the iterative continuation task and the comparative continuation task have been carried out to verify their effectiveness. The studies on the former show its effects on lowering language errors (Zhang & Zhang, 2019) and improving writing fluency and accuracy (Miao & Wang, 2022), and the studies on the latter show its effects on alignment of words and phrases (Xiong, 2018) and lowering L2 writing anxiety (Pu et al., 2022).

The continuation task has been widely implemented to enhance L2 learning effect. A number of studies have been conducted to explore its effects from different perspectives. On the linguistic level, the continuation task is effective in improving the learner's language accuracy and syntaxic and discoursal complexity (Jiang & Chen, 2015; Mao & Jiang, 2017; Xin & Li, 2020). In terms of language areas, studies have shown that the continuation task significantly enhances the acquisition of L2 vocabulary, such as articles, quantifiers and specialized words (Hong & Shi, 2016; Wang & Wang, 2016; Xu & Wang, 2020), L2 grammar such as subjunctive mood, relative clause, verb-resultative construction, etc. (Xin, 2017; Wang & Wang, 2019; Liu & Wang, 2018), and L2 discourse such as coherence and rhetoric (Miao, 2017; Peng, 2017; Yang, 2018). On the psychological level, the continuation task has been found to be effective in enhancing L2 learners' learning agency (Zhang & Zhang, 2021) and attitude and lowering their writing anxiety (Zhang

& Qin, 2020) and reliance on L1 (Jiang et al., 2019).

The main factors that influence the effectiveness of the continuation task include input characteristics (e.g. language type, length, complexity, genre, topic, etc.), task conditions (e.g. requirement on content creation, instruction on language, use of interaction, prompt, etc.) and learner factors (e.g. motivation, anxiety, willingness to communicate, L2 proficiency, use of L1 thinking, etc.). These factors should be carefully considered when the continuation task is used to enhance L2 acquisition.

The xu-argument has had a huge impact on foreign language teaching and learning in China. It provides a new perspective for understanding the mechanism of language acquisition: alignment between input and output. Alignment is learning and is realized through continuation, which activates the various external and internal factors facilitating language acquisition. The continuation task has been adopted in high-stake English tests, such as the college entrance examination, which prompts language teachers to apply the xu-argument to foreign language teaching. Most practitioners have applauded the continuation task for its effect on achieving high efficiency in teaching a language.

Theoretically, acknowledging the interactionist approach to second language acquisition, the xu-argument contends that interaction is driven by xu, or continuation, extension and creation, without which interaction wouldn't occur. It points to a new direction for language acquisition research and the xu-based research has been carried about to test its principles through continuation tasks. The xu-argument views language learning as creative imitation where imitation of language use co-occurs with the creation of ideas driven by the comprehension-production asymmetry (Wang, 2021). Comprehension-production asymmetry is continuously ironed out by making one's production align with what is comprehended from the input, and that is language learning.

2.3 Innovation of the Production-Oriented Approach (POA)

2.3.1 Construction of POA

To address the weaknesses in English instruction in Chinese higher education, Wen and colleagues have endeavored to develop a teaching theory that can enhance college English teaching effect and improve students' ability to use English in communicative contexts. The Production-Oriented Approach (POA) has been proposed as a comprehensive L2 pedagogy based on the status quo of L2 learning in China. L2 learning, especially English learning has been found to be inadequate in developing students' communicative ability due to the overemphasis on learning language knowledge. The problem has essentially lain in the separation of learning and using the language which the POA seeks to address.

The POA initially based its construction on the output hypothesis which stresses the important role of output in SLA. Reacting to the claim about the essential role of comprehensible input, Swain (1985) argues that it is comprehensible output that can improve both fluency and accuracy in the interlanguage of the L2 learner. As Swain states, the learner can stretch his or her interlanguage to meet communicative goals and the need to produce the target language serves as a trigger to draw the learner's attention to means of conveying his or her intended meaning. From a psycholinguistic point of view, output has a number of functions. Firstly, output facilitates the development of L2 automaticity, which refers to fluency in language use. Secondly, output helps the learner to test his or her hypotheses about the target language against feedback received from the interlocutor. Thirdly, output helps the learner to control and reflect on their language use, thus serving a metalinguistic function. Finally, output helps the learner to notice the gap between what they want to say and what they can say, prompting him or her to attend to relevant information in the input and leading to L2 development (Izumi, 2003). Though the POA acknowledges the importance of output, it uses the term production instead, which includes not only speaking and writing, but also translating and interpreting. Besides, production emphasizes both "producing" and "product". What's more, the POA mainly targets tertiary-level English learners while the output hypothesis doesn't distinguish learners (Wen, 2015).

The text-centered English teaching method in Chinese higher education tends to separate learning from language use, leading to the problem of "high investment and low effectiveness". The POA, incorporating the output-driven hypothesis (ODH), input-enabled hypothesis (IEH) and selective-learning hypothesis (SLH), has been developed to overcome this problem. The POA is said to enable learners to undertake genuine communicative tasks that are in line with their English proficiency (Wen, 2016).

Based on the POA, L2 learning starts with productive activities and ends with productive activities. That is what the ODH is concerning. Students try out a productive activity before resorting to enabling materials so that they will notice what they lack in performing the activity and become more engaged in learning the enabling materials. The IEH holds that the carefully designed reading or listening materials will enable the students to approach their zones of proximal development, which is essential for efficient L2 learning. The SLH assumes that in the process of learning the enabling materials, students can selectively process what is needed to fulfill the productive activity, such as relevant ideas, linguistic expressions or discourse features, leading to better learning outcomes.

The POA diverges on the widely shared assumption that learning begins with input followed by output, and places output before input to serve as a driving force for L2 learning. Actually, the POA is more concerned with the order of pedagogical activities than the order of L2 learning. Following the POA, teaching procedures consist of three phases: motivating, enabling and assessing. The teacher plays a mediating role in all three phases. The motivating phase is related to the ODH. The teacher makes explicit the scenario of the communicative task and the students try out the productive activity, followed by the teacher's explanation of the learning objectives, both the communicative and linguistic objectives. The enabling phase is related to the IEH and SLH, and is the essential part of the POA. The teacher guides the students step-by-step to expand their knowledge base and their linguistic systems through suitable enabling materials, so that they can fulfill the assigned productive activity. The assessing phase can be divided into two parts: ongoing formative assessment and achievement assessment. The teacher needs to set up criteria for assessing learning outcomes jointly with the students. Both the teacher and the students should be involved in the assessment, where the teacher can provide feedback and guide revisions and the students can review their own learning process.

The POA has been proposed against the backdrop of urgent need for constructing foreign language teaching theories with Chinese characteristics. Although the POA drew upon the well-established western SLA theories, such as the output hypothesis, it fully considered the status quo of foreign language teaching in the Chinese context and developed a theoretical system for teaching foreign languages in China. The innovative aspects of the POA are four-folds. Firstly, it integrates foreign language pedagogy and SLA theories. There has long been a gap between the two, so Ellis and Shintani (2014) suggest connecting them through two routes. The first route is to have foreign language teachers apply SLA research findings to their teaching, and the second route is to have SLA theorists examine language pedagogy. Wen (2020) argues that the two connecting routes won't effectively bridge the gap. Instead, the POA better links language pedagogy and SLA theories, as all the POA teaching phases employ language pedagogy informed by SLA theories. For example, the enabling phase has its teaching objectives, content, method and assessment, which are informed by the output-driven hypothesis and selective learning hypothesis. Secondly, the POA has been continuously modified based on feedback of teaching practice. Since the very beginning, the POA theorists have been involved in the relevant teaching preparation and closely followed the teaching process in order to improve the validity and feasibility of the POA. Thirdly, the POA has been developed to solve the separation of language learning and using, a problem commonly seen in foreign language classrooms in China. Foreign language classrooms devoted most of the time to text-centered learning and receptive skill training, resulting in limited training of learners' productive ability. After realizing the limitation, language teachers attempted to give students more language use opportunities through tasks or projects. However, only by increasing opportunities and not providing necessary scaffolds, teachers couldn't effectively improve students' productive ability as students often still struggled with production difficulties. The POA responds to this situation by not only increasing production opportunities but also addressing production difficulties head-on. Finally, the POA emphasizes the role of the teacher instead of marginalizing the teacher amid calls for learner-centeredness since the 1990s. The expertise of the teacher is indispensable to maximizing the learning effect of the students. Therefore, the POA challenges the learner-centered principle and proposes the learning-centered principle, which focuses on activating the learning instead of the learner as a person (Wen, 2016). Instruction should be carefully planned, organized and implemented by the teacher to achieve high teaching efficiency and learning effect.

The POA has been studied empirically and proved effective in improving teaching efficiency and learning effect. Zhang Lingli (2017) adopted POA in teaching college English and found that the students' motivation for learning English was enhanced and their listening and writing skills were significantly improved. Zhang Wenjuan (2017)'s study also showed that POA was effective in improving students' language proficiency and language use in writing. Wen (2018) explored the motivating phase of the POA and found it could enhance the students' motivation for learning new knowledge and willingness to use language.

2.3.2 Design of POA activities

Motivating activities

Studies (e.g. Yang, 2015, Shao, 2019) showed how the motivating phase could be realized and what principles should be followed, which would enlighten the design of the POA motivating phase. The students may be directly or indirectly motivated. At the motivating phase, the communicative tasks should be authentic, cognitively challenging and meeting appropriate production objectives. Wen (2020) stresses the importance of clarifying production scenario in the motivating phase design and details the scenario elements, including topic, purpose, identity and context. Appropriate production scenarios contain potential communication value while inappropriate scenarios have limited effect on motivating the students to communicate. Here is an example of production scenario for the instruction on the topic of Chinese food:

You and your classmates invite your foreign teacher for lunch at a nearby restaurant. Dumplings are usually very popular with foreigners, so you order them for her and then she asks you a number of questions about how to make them. You are going to describe the procedures of making dumplings so that she can do it by herself. (Wen, 2020)

Enabling activities

The enabling phase manifests the input-enabled hypothesis and the selective-learning hypothesis. It includes three steps: 1) the teacher explains sub-activities of production; 2) the teacher guides the students to complete selective learning and enabling activities; 3) the teacher guides the students to complete production. In this process, it's essential that the teacher provide scaffolds that fit the students' proficiency levels. It's theorized that the enabling activities should be gradual, aligned and varied to ensure effectiveness (Wen, 2017). To be specific, the activities should advance gradually with necessary scaffolds, align with the production objectives and difficulties, and have variety of information channels and activity forms. Qiu (2017) designed the teaching procedure of enabling activities and explored their effect through a teaching experiment. She organized the tasks by complexity from the cognitive and linguistic dimensions. By investigating 8 students, she concluded that the careful design of enabling activities facilitated better acquisition of target language, thus meeting the POA teaching objectives.

Qiu (2019) further explored the enabling phase by adopting the dialectical research method where she conducted three cycles of research that focused on gradual enabling, aligned enabling and varied enabling respectively. She arrived at a refined theoretical framework, better teaching strategies and sound explanation of the enabling phase.

Teacher-Student Collaborative Assessment

Assessment is a critical phase of language teaching. Research has confirmed that all kinds of assessment are largely beneficial, particularly when the instructor is involved. In the Chinese culture, teachers are highly respected and students usually take their assessment seriously, thus responding actively and making progress. The POA theorists adopted the mode of teacher-student collaborative assessment (TSCA) as an innovative assessment method to organize and balance teacher assessment and other types of assessments (Wen, 2016). It is said to contain three distinct features. First, TSCA doesn't equate with teacher assessment plus student assessment. It is a kind of dynamic assessment where the teacher guides the students to make constant collaborative assessments during the process of learning. In that way, assessment and learning are naturally integrated rather than being separate tasks. Second, assessment is not made merely on the products of learning, but on whether the learning objectives are met. Usually the POA incorporates language objectives and communicative objectives, thus the assessment is oriented toward these objectives. Third, TSCA is not confined to in-class assessment where the teacher guides the students to assess their performance in production tasks. In addition, the teacher needs to select and assess a few samples before class and students need to conduct further self or peer assessment after class, followed by automated assessment and teacher assessment (Wen, 2020). TSCA is an indispensable part of the POA, supporting and advancing the motivating and enabling phases. Sun (2017) explored viable guidelines for TSCA and possible ways of realizing TSCA. Through reflective teaching practice, she proposed a set of guidelines for deciding assessment focus and suggested strategies to ensure assessment for learning. The students' attitude toward TSCA was quite positive, as they gained new perception of and new progress through assessment for learning.

2.3.3 Research on POA

To validate the POA, the theorists proposed the dialectical research method (DRM) which has its basis on both dialectical materialism and western research tradition. As an instructed SLA theory, the POA focuses more on the efficiency of language teaching than the necessity and sufficiency of language acquisition. Therefore, conventional SLA research methods, such as experiments, may not work for the research of the POA while DRM can better meet the needs of instructed SLA research.

The theoretical framework of DRM is composed of the philosophy, research process as well as data collection and analysis method. Wen (2017) takes instructed SLA as a complex system which includes hierarchical layers of various subsystems, and believes that research should consider the multi-factors in the system and explore how the interrelations among them affect language teaching effect. However, many studies don't adopt a system perspective but endeavor to identify some simple causal relations which don't reflect what instructed SLA truly is. DRM also emphasizes the importance of practice and holds that theory derives from practice and is tested by practice.

DRM includes four elements: question, theory, practice and self-reflection. The question should come from the researcher's real experience instead of reviewing literature. Neither is the question from minor problems that represent only part of the classroom teaching. Instead, the question of DRM is directly oriented toward the key issue, the theory should be empirical and operational. The practice is informed by the theory and can offer constructive feedback to the improvement of the theory. DRM is also open to and interact with others' theory and practice based on self-reflection, resulting in the improvement of the current theory. DRM involves a complete cycle of research process consisting of the four elements. The process can be cyclic and continual with more questions, theories, practices and reflections. DRM is particularly suitable for researching the POA which aims to address the key issues of instructed SLA.

DRM employs diverse methods to collect different kinds of data. There are three main types of data to be collected: 1) observations; 2) self-reports; 3) learning outcomes. For observation data, class video-recording and observation can be used to examine the behavior of the teacher and students. For self-reporting data, questionnaires, interviews and learning journals can be used to detect the feelings and perceptions of the subjects that cannot be directly observed. Learning outcomes can be spoken and written products or language proficiency test performance. DRM advocates tracking data so that student portfolios can be created to reflect teaching effect. The first two types of data are mainly analyzed qualitatively, and quantitative analysis of questionnaires can obtain additional results. The learning outcomes can be analyzed using different methods to explore different dimensions. There may be cross-sectional and longitudinal data of language products and test performance that need to be compared in order to understand the teaching effect on language acquisition.

The POA theorists have been using DRM to formulate theory through practice. There have been four rounds of theory-practice interactive research, and the hypotheses have been gradually modified and the newest version of POA theory system has been eventually formulated (Wen, 2017). The theorists have also pondered over how to adjust DRM because "method" is too narrow to describe what DRM encompasses. They decided to change DRM to dialectical research paradigm (DRP). Paradigm refers to the common beliefs held by the academic community regarding ontology, epistemology and methodology. DRP, based on the dialectical relationship between theory and practice, aims at solving complex, critical and systematic problems through multiple rounds of cyclic research.

2.3.4 Critique of POA

The POA has contributed to the development of applied linguistics in China. Admittedly, the POA has much in common with the well-established approach – task-based language teaching (TBLT), such as "the whole-person education" and "learning by doing". However, the POA has some obvious strengths in foreign language teaching in China. First, the POA can be applied to formal English teaching in Chinese higher education where large numbers of students take the course mostly to improve their English proficiency in the academic context. Second, the POA stresses the integration of learning and using and the dynamic relationship between input and output, which can solve the problem low learning efficiency and limited productive ability of the students. Third, the POA links SLA theories with language teaching practice. The hypotheses proposed by the POA are informed by SLA theories and at the same time enlighten pedagogical practice (Deng, 2018).

Some scholars may have concerns about the POA's disregard for learners' interactive competence (Wen, 2020). From the design of teaching phrases, we can see that much emphasis is given to how input enables production, particularly written output. However, interactive skills, such as negotiation of meaning, are not rarely discussed in the POA. For the POA to become a well-grounded instructed SLA theory, it's important for the theorists to explore means to cultivating learners' interactive competence. In addition, teacher's guidance is essential in the POA, which may restrain learners' creativity. Critical thinking and creativity are critical skills that higher education aims to develop in the students. Over emphasis on meeting language and communicative objectives squeeze out the space for other important objectives. How to balance the teacher's guidance and giving the students opportunities to develop creativity is what the POA theorists need to address in future research.

Chapter Three Innovation in Content of Foreign Language Learning and Teaching

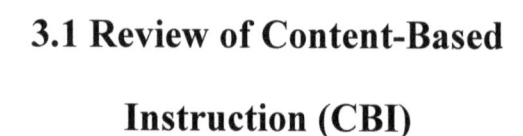

3.1 Review of Content-Based Instruction (CBI)

Following the promotion of Content-Based Instruction (CBI), researchers and practitioners have developed different types of instruction that are along the continuum of CBI. For example, English-medium instruction focuses almost entirely on content teaching with limited or no attention to language teaching, while the other end of continuum focuses overwhelmingly on language teaching with content playing a marginal role.

Research has supported the integration of attention to language form with attention to content knowledge as an effective combination in learning. Still, it's hard to know how learners of different proficiency levels achieve the balanced attention to both learning targets. For language learners, especially foreign language majors, the primary goal is to develop language knowledge and skills. That's not to say, CBI should be abandoned. As a pedagogical development of communicative language teaching (CLT) approach, CBI in SL/FL has solid theoretical foundations. CLT marks the outset of a paradigm shift of language teaching in the twentieth century. The shift of attention from language competence to communicative competence in the 1970s made an ideational and notional syllabus a better choice than a structuralist syllabus. Chomsky (1965)'s generative theory has a central assumption that language is represented as a speaker's mental grammar, which is termed "competence". Language competence focuses on language correctness or accuracy, and learners are expected to demonstrate rule-governed language use (grammatical competence) without concerns for appropriate use of language in context. Hymes (1972) extended Chomsky's language competence to include sociolinguistic and pragmatic factors, which was referred to as "communicative competence". It includes both grammatical competence and pragmatic competence. Hymes' communicative competence and Halliday (1973)'s systemic-functional grammar laid the linguistic foundations for CLT. In addition, Krashen (1982)'s monitor theory pointed out a second language could be acquired through exposure to comprehensible input. Thus, CLT developed to emphasize meaningful use of language with the focus on message and fluency.

CBI can be considered as a logical development of CLT, both having core principles regarding the role of meaning in language teaching. CBI is widely used in English-speaking countries to prepare ESL students for elementary, secondary and tertiary education. "Content" has become a buzzword in language teaching since the 1990s. It usually refers to substance or the subject matter that we learn or communicate through language. CBI, therefore, is the teaching of subject matter "in the language being learned with little or no direct or explicit effort to teach the language itself separately from the content being taught" (Krahnke, 1987, p.65). Language that is used to present subject matter is a by-product of learning about the real-world content. CBI has much association with some curriculum designs in native-language education in the UK and the US, which advocated the combination of languages skills and content subjects that required the collaboration between subject teachers and language teachers. Moreover, there were both subject matter and language teaching goals. CBI has also been influenced by immersion education which is a type of foreign language instruction in which subject courses are taught through the foreign language. Another area associated with CBI is language for specific purposes (e.g. ESP) that intends to serve the needs of learners who need the language for their specific roles such as engineers, technicians, nurses, etc., or who need the language to acquire knowledge or real-world skills. CBI courses were originally carried out in native language curriculum designs and ESL programs and later adopted by EFL courses around the world.

Content areas that are attractive in nature should be considered for CBI, because the students can more effectively acquire a second language when they are motivated by communicating ideas in that language. In addition, content that meets the needs of students is often used in CBI courses. The spoken and written texts that students will encounter in the real world can be selected for these courses. Likewise, if the materials build on students' knowledge and previous experience, i.e. content that the students already know, they serve as ideal learning materials in CBI courses.

In CBI courses, language use depends on integrated skills. For example, students may engage in reading a text and writing a summary, or respond orally to things they have listened to. The theme-based courses provide coherence across the skill areas and focus on language use in connected discourse. Grammar is regarded as a component of these skills or a complement to theme-based activities, and is not usually treated as a separate dimension. The basic assumption of CBI is that language acquisition is incidental to learning about the content. However, the meaning-focused language instruction has been debated ever since the introduction of CLT and CBI, as researchers have found that good content learning may not always bring about good language learning (Swain, 1988). For learners who don't have enough exposure to language, it's quite unlikely that they acquire high levels of second language proficiency through meaning-focused instruction. Instead, they seem to benefit from form-focused instruction although some SLA researchers have argued that instruction that focuses on language itself brings marginal benefit if not negative effect (Krashen, 1994; Truscott, 1999). However, other empirical studies have found positive results of form-focused instruction in CBI in the aspects of L2 fluency and accuracy (Spada & Lightbown, 1993; Lyster, 2004). There has been a consensus that "instruction is most effective when it includes attention to both form and meaning" (Spada & Lightbown, 2008).

3.2 Review of Content and Language Integrated Learning (CLIL)

While CBI treats language acquisition as a by-product of learning content knowledge, Content Language Integrated Learning (CLIL) has been developed to focus on both language acquisition and content knowledge. CLIL was launched in Europe in the 1990s as a response to the need for second language education and bilingualism. CLIL advocates a 50-50 content-language equilibrium, which distinguishes it from CBI. In reality, it's difficult to achieve a strict balance between content and language. As a result, there is a wide range of combinations of content and language that can be put under the umbrella term of CLIL, which causes some scholars to question the conceptualization of CLIL.

There are a number of features about CLIL that

make it distinguishable from other language teaching approaches. The language goal of CLIL is somewhat controversial. Some scholars claim that CLIL doesn't expect the learners to achieve native-like proficiency, while some research found very high language levels were required of the students in CLIL programs. Nevertheless, CLIL is said to be suitable for a broad range of learners and able to function in all learning contexts, thus advocating an egalitarian approach to language teaching (Marsh, 2002). As a content-driven language teaching approach different from other types of approaches such as CBI, it extends the experience of learning a language. What is innovative about CLIL is that it often draws on academic content, and that explains why CLIL develops high-order language skills. CLIL adopts a systematic integration of language and content, which cannot be seen in other approaches. However, it's argued that these characteristics of CLIL are also possessed by CBI. For example, CBI is also claimed to be content-driven instead of language-driven (Met, 1998) and educators have paid attention to systematic and coherent integration of language and content in immersion programs (Swain 1996; Lyster 2007). Despite the attempt of CLIL experts to stress its uniqueness, CLIL educators have acknowledged the implications of immersion programs (a common type of CBI) for the development of CLIL methodology. A categorical distinction between CLIL and CBI is difficult to make, thus both should be treated as umbrella terms that cover a wide variety of teaching alternatives and learning opportunities with content and language integration (CENOZ et. al., 2014).

3.3 Innovation in Content and Language Integration (CLI)

In the Chinese context, there have long been

skepticisms about curriculum design for English majors that is oriented toward developing language skills. Some of the main problems associated with this orientation are limited discipline knowledge and weak critical thinking skills of students. According to the national curriculum for English as a specialty, students should not only master the English language skills, but also acquire a certain amount of knowledge in relevant disciplines, and comprehensive abilities and qualities. However, the skill-oriented instruction has traditionally dominated such courses as English speaking, listening, reading and writing usually offered to first and second-year students although a few knowledge-based courses are provided to third-year students (Chang & Xia, 2011). Obviously, the objectives set by the national curriculum can hardly be achieved by continuing the traditional instruction. When endeavoring to carry out reforms, English educators in China have been enlightened by CBI as a new approach to language teaching. CBI holds out promise for a dual-functional pedagogy that promotes language skills and content knowledge at the same time. CBI was introduced to China in the 1990s, but its application in English teaching wasn't implemented until after 2000. A number of empirical studies were published to show the positive effects of CBI on students' language proficiency, disciplinary knowledge, and critical thinking ability. Chang, Zhao and Li (2008) proposed an innovative CBI curriculum for English majors that took into consideration the guidelines of CBI and the objectives of the national curriculum for English as a specialty, as well as students' needs and teachers' academic backgrounds. Later, an empirical study was conducted to examine the effects of the new curriculum on students' development of English language skills and disciplinary knowledge (Chang & Xia, 2011). The results indicate positive effects on both areas, which provides implications for teaching reforms enlightened by CBI. Chang (2020) subsequently proposed a localized approach called Content and Language Integration (CLI). The integration of content and language is not based on a rigid proportion, but rather implemented flexibly according to stages of language learning. For example, in the earlier stage when students' language proficiency is relatively low, more emphasis should be put on teaching language skills than on imparting disciplinary knowledge in a certain course. CLI is claimed to expand the curriculum to incorporate systematic disciplinary knowledge so English-major students can receive adequate education to become well-rounded individuals. The approach has also been reflected in the national standards for cultivating English majors, and has been adopted by foreign language departments of universities around the country.

In the English department of my university,

teaching reforms have been carried out to better cultivate students' comprehensive abilities. The curriculum was reformed to include more courses that are content driven, such as Chinese Culture, American Culture, British Culture, English Literature, English Linguistics, Cross-Culture Communication, International Relations, International Trade, etc. Besides, the skill-oriented courses were reformed to incorporate content area knowledge from disciplines like linguistics, literature, sociology, philosophy, etc. The purpose of these reforms was to improve English-major students' language proficiency, disciplinary knowledge, and high-order thinking skills. Foreign language educators consider the above mentioned disciplines essential for English majors as they comprise core areas of humanities. Having a touch with them can definitely benefit liberal arts students in their way of thinking and overall quality desired by our society.

Tasks were also designed in ways that they could take advantage of the content and language integration. They were no longer directed merely toward language skills and language knowledge, but rather the mastery of skills and knowledge that would make them well-rounded individuals. The non-linguistic skills can include interpersonal communication, autonomous and cooperative learning. One special task called project-based learning (PBL) was often used in the content-and-language-integration courses. Students formed small groups to explore topics relating to the target content using the target language. PBL has been proved to be an effective language learning method in different contexts. In the process of PBL, students cooperated with each other to examine authentic questions or solve read world problems, which requires them to make use of language, knowledge and skills in their repertoire. This type of project serves as an effective task in content-and-language-integration courses, as it links the content and language in a natural and meaningful way. The outcome oriented nature of PBL also makes students responsible for their own learning, improving their learning strategies and preparing them for life-long learning. The assessment of PBL could not only reflect language skills, disciplinary knowledge, but also critical thinking ability and interpersonal skills, which are not easily observable in other types of tasks. PBL as an innovative pedagogical practice in China will be elaborated in one of the following chapters.

The uniqueness of content and language integration practices in China lies in the consideration of broader goals than the original CBI and CLIL would expect. The CLI takes into account the characteristics of EFL in the Chinese context and develops curriculum, pedagogy, teaching materials and tasks that are in line with the goals associated with cultivating well-rounded foreign language talents.

When it comes to the content in English teaching and learning, more and more attention is paid to areas that meet the social needs for talents. This has always been true since English became a popular major in the 1980s. The popularity of English was very much due to the reform and opening-up policy initiated in 1978. With the increasing needs for international business and communication, almost all the Chinese universities started to set up English departments. English education was directed towards producing English speakers and translators that could be put into use quickly. Thus, English skills became the primary goals in English education. While skill training continued to occupy the central position over the years, more and more attention was directed toward ability development. A number of English educators raised questions and criticisms about the existing curricula when it was found that large numbers of students graduated with mediocre qualifications. The questions and criticisms were mainly concerned with students' inadequate knowledge base and limited critical thinking ability, which in turn compelled the English departments to make changes to their curriculums and teaching methods. Among the reforms, content and language integration has been systematically designed, implemented and researched.

Influenced by the advocacy of New Liberal Arts, which is among the "Four News" currently promoted in Chinese Higher Education, reforms in foreign language as a discipline have been widely discussed and implemented to meet the requirements of higher quality development. In 2019, the Ministry of Education of China proposed the construction of "Four News", namely New Engineering, New Medicine, New Agriculture and New Liberal Arts, to address the challenges brought by the new round of technological and industrial revolutions by cultivating talents that would lead in the revolutions. According to educators and researchers, New Liberal Arts requirements will directly impact the construction of the foreign language discipline. The skills, knowledge, abilities and qualities of foreign language majors are specified. Skills of using the target language accurately, fluently and appropriately are still stressed as has been before. What kind of knowledge and abilities should be possessed by foreign language students is often debated. For English majors, it's said that the knowledge of the English language and culture, literature, translation and English countries and regions is essential. With regard to the knowledge of English countries and regions, special attention should be paid to their history, society, culture, religion, politics, economic and technological developments. Besides, the students should also possess enough knowledge of their own country in the above-mentioned aspects

(Huang, 2022). As for abilities, English majors should have English and Chinese language use ability, literary appreciation ability, interpretation and translation, cross-cultural ability, critical thinking ability, learning ability, information technology use ability, creative ability, research ability, etc. Overall, reforms are directed toward cultivating well-rounded talents through integration of disciplines of liberal arts and even other disciplines, such as information technology. Apart from New Liberal Arts, there are still some attempts to integrate the foreign language discipline with others among the "Four News". To take an example of integration with New Agriculture, in agriculture universities students can enroll in programs that integrate English linguistics and ecology. Actually, foreign language majors are encouraged to make full use of the specialty of their universities and construct specialized programs that will distinguish their graduates from others'.

Content and Language Integration intends to solve the problem of producing low achievers in language or in discipline knowledge. Therefore, it's considered an education approach not limited to teaching and learning a foreign language, but cultivating well-rounded foreign language talents.

Chapter Four Innovation in Multimodal Foreign Language Teaching

4.1 Review of multimodal pedagogy

Multimodal research has received much attention in the Western academia since the 1990s, and has been a hot topic in China in the new century. Multimodality is defined as using different modes (visual, aural, textual, spatial and others) for communication or meaning-making (Kress, 2016). Multimodality focuses on how semiotic resources work and are organized. Most of the theories and analyses on multimodality are informed by systemic functional linguistics and its offshoot social semiotics. Kress (2010) claims that multimodality should be taken as a normal state of communication and contemporary learning is to deal with a world of meaning which is characterized as being multimodal. O'Halloran et al. (2016) point out the digital technology has revolutionized higher education to increasingly recognize the need to develop multimodal competencies of students.

There has been a growing interest in the pedagogical application of multimodality in the field of SLA. Researchers advocate the implementation of multimodal pedagogy in language teaching and studies have shown that English learners improve their multi-literacy skills, enhance learning motivation and autonomy through multimodal practice. Stein (2000) proposed multimodal pedagogy by conceptualizing classrooms as semiotic spaces where learners who are the agents of their own meaning making produce multimodal texts. Teachers should recognize the limits of language and try to make full use of semiotic resources in the classroom, including language, gesture, sounds, images, silences, etc. An important aim of multimodal pedagogy is multimodal literacy, defined as the ability to construct meanings through "reading, viewing, understanding, responding to and producing and interacting with multimedia and digital texts" (Walsh, 2010, p. 213). Multimodal literacy has been relevant for language teaching as practitioners come to realize that they need to help learners to exploit semiotic modes to understand and produce the target language more effectively. Researchers are particularly interested in how non-verbal elements reinforce or add meaning to verbal expressions and how multimodal approaches can motivate learners. Studies have verified the advantages of using techniques and resources that highlight multimodality in the support of meaning making (Camiciottoli & Cubillo, 2018).

In SLA, proficiency is a key word, which typically focuses on the linguistic dimension. However, there is a growing awareness of the importance of fostering multimodal literacy in the language teaching contexts (Royce & Bowcher, 2007). There are discussions on the research relating to the four skills (speaking, listening, writing, and reading) that has drawn on multimodality as the underlying conceptual framework (Camiciottoli & Cubillo, 2018). Strategies for multimodal reading proposed by Liu (2013) were initially used for interpreting images, but may also be needed for comprehending other modes. Liu's multimodal strategy framework can inspire the development of educational models that can promote multimodal literacy and assess students' performance in this regard. As for writing, it's found that using visual mode facilitates the learners' production of well-structured and logically flowing texts (Stein, 2000). The multimodal approach to L2 writing leads to the students' creation of texts that combine multiple modes, that is, multimodal composition (Selfe, 2007), which is found to be an effective way to motivate the students to learn English as they actively engage with multimodal digital resources (Street et al., 2011). Listening effectively is key in all kinds of relationships and in all kinds of communicative contexts. In multimodal environments, understanding non-verbal information is an essential part of the listening experience. Similarly, effective oral communication involves not only language proficiency, but also non-verbal knowledge and skills. When developing speaking skills, learners need the awareness of the contribution of non-verbal elements in communication. The most effective way to raise speaking proficiency is to practice using non-verbal elements while speaking.

4.2 Innovation in multimodal foreign language teaching in China

Research on multimodal foreign language teaching in China has gradually mounted up with increasing influence of modern media technology. Chinese scholars, Li Zhanzi, Hu Zhuanglin, Gu Yueguo, are among the first to have studied multimodality in foreign language teaching. Li (2003) points out the positive impact of multimodal discourse analysis on English teaching. Hu (2007) distinguishes between multimodal semiotics and multimedia semiotics and emphasizes the importance of developing multiliteracies. Gu (2007) differentiates multimodal learning from multimedia learning, and constructs an analytic model to dissect the two kinds of learning.

Zhang Delu is one of the pioneering researchers on multimodal foreign language teaching in China. His research has both theoretical and practical significance and is rich in innovations. Zhang (2009) developed a framework for multimodal discourse analysis and research that could guide the choice of effective procedures and practice in foreign language teaching supported by modern media technology. He suggested that the choice of modes be made by taking into consideration three conditions: 1) the modes can provide new learning environment; 2) the modes can provide enabling conditions; 3) the modes can provide multi-channels for meaning-making. Zhang (2010) investigated the concept of design in the selection of modalities in foreign language classroom teaching. Design in multimodal discourse means the conscious selection of modes for the construction of reality. It's a process of creating discourse and interpreting discourse and a process of using all possible resources to engage in communication. Design is especially important for the use of new media. To realize design in teaching practice, he discussed the possible stages, steps and methods involved in the teaching. Principles of the selection of modes systems based on design were also proposed. The principle of effectiveness means that the selection of modes should be directed toward the presentation of the best results. The principle of adaptation emphasizes that when multiple modes are used together, the selection criterion is to obtain the best combination. The principle of economy states that the simpler the selection of modes, the better. These principles provide rational reference for teachers when choosing modes in foreign language teaching. Zhang & Wang (2010) investigated how different modes coordinate to achieve the teaching objectives of College English classroom teaching in China. Through two cases, they found that the main mode is oral language, highlighted and complemented by other modes such as PowerPoint slides, blackboard writing and body language. They also proposed several suggestions for language teachers to improve teaching through better coordinating the different modes in the classroom.

Recent studies have advocated a multiliteracies approach over traditional literacy practices (Thwaites, 1999) and multiliteracies have been increasingly adopted as a teaching objective of multimodal pedagogy. The previous understanding of literacy has been replaced by the notion of literacy as multiple, layered and social. Practices of creating meaning and making meaning are inherently dynamic, multimodal and culturally diverse. Adopting a multiliteracies perspective has proved significant in literacy teaching and learning practices. The New London Group (1996) called for a broader view of literacy than portrayed by traditional language-based approaches and discussed how a multiliteracies pedagogical model might engage students to design their social futures in a culturally and linguistically diverse world. The researchers of the group proposed six design elements of the meaning-making process (i.e. linguistic design, visual design, audio design, gestural design, spatial design, and multimodal design) and four components of pedagogy (situated practice, overt instruction, critical framing, and transformed practice). In the L2 classroom, situated practice is authentic activities that provides learners with immersive experience relating to their real life and meeting their emotional and social needs, so that they are interested in taking part in them. Overt instruction is to provide scaffolds to students when they are learning new content, which helps them develop metalanguage for understanding the internal relations of different kinds of knowledge in a specific system. Critical framing aims at helping students to link what they've learned in situated practice and overt instruction with the society, history, culture and values in social practice, so that they can critically evaluate the systematic knowledge and creatively apply it in a broader context. Transformed practice enables students to apply what they've learned in the previous stages in new situations.

The pedagogical components have much in common with the pedagogical practices of experiencing, conceptualizing, analyzing, and applying, later conceptualized by two of the researchers in the group. To be specific, when experiencing, students relate to what they already know and interpret new situations or texts. When conceptualizing, students compare, contrast, and generalize. When analyzing, students explore causes and effects. When applying, students design new meaning in real-world situations, often through digital multimodal projects (Cope & Kalantzis, 2009).

Zhang (2012) elaborated what multiliteracies to develop and how to develop them in foreign language learners. First, linguistic literacy is essential for L2 learners. However, it's different from the traditional approach to literacy in that it emphases learners' ability to recognize linguistic meaning potential and to use other modes to coordinate with the linguistic mode in meaning-making. Second, social communication literacy, which includes cultural literacy, political literacy, critical literacy and postmodern literacy (Thwaites, 1999). Cultural literacy incorporates relevant knowledge such as social knowledge, ethical standards and principles, etc. Political literacy requires students to have mature political quality, master knowledge related to politics, and have the ability to interpret political phenomena. Critical literacy is the ability to evaluate the selected modality and the meaning of expression. The postmodern literacy advocates deconstructionism, emphasizes variability, uniqueness, heterogeneity, and diversity, and opposes using norms and laws to understand things. Third, technical literacy is required of L2 learners, which means L2 learners need to possess scientific literacy and media literacy. Mastering knowledge and skills of modern media technology is necessary but not enough; understanding the various modes and their meaning potential is also important for L2 learners. It's argued that these literacies can be developed by following the four pedagogical steps proposed by the New London Group (1996): situated practice, overt instruction, critical framing, and transformed practice. However, the steps are not sequential or hierarchical, but interactional and flexible according to specific teaching plans. Figure 1 shows the procedure of the teaching steps. The order of situated practice and overt instruction is decided by the teaching context. When the learning content is difficult, overt instruction should be conducted first. When the teaching focus is on skill training, situated practice can take place first, followed by overt instruction. Critical framing is included as a teaching step so that the students can objectively review and critically evaluate what they have learned at an individual or social distance, and then creatively apply it. Transformed practice provides the students with opportunities to apply what they have learned in new contexts.

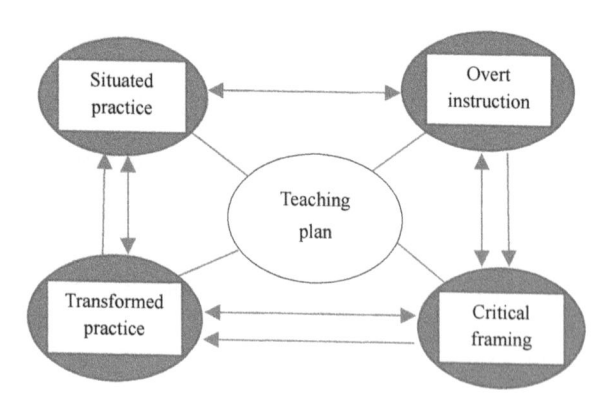

Figure 1. Teaching Procedure of Multiliteracies

Drawing on the multiliteracies pedagogy, Zhang and Ding (2013) put forward the framework of mode choice in multimodal foreign language teaching. The researchers identified the foreign language teaching genre structure which include 9 obligatory components and 7 optional components. The obligatory components are: Class Beginning, Teaching Objective, Main Content, Situated Experiencing, Conceptualisation & Theorisation, Discussion & Debate, Practice & Application, Assignments, Finish. The optional components are: Pre-class Activity, Teaching Requirements, Review, Background Information; Question & Discussion, Interpretation & Evaluation, Summary. Among them, four components (Situated Experiencing, Conceptualisation & Theorisation, Discussion & Debate, Practice & Application) constitute the obligatory components of a multiliteracies model of foreign language teaching. Learning by design is considered the core concept of the multiliteracies model that facilitates the realization of teaching objectives. Design emphasizes that meaning-making is an active and dynamic process. Design involves three elements: Available Designs, Designing and The Redesigned. Available Designs are the Design resources from which we make meaning, Designing means the process of shaping meaning which involves the transformation of Available Designs, and The Resigned is the outcome of Designing, a new and transformed meaning. In practice, teachers need to choose appropriate teaching methods and modes to assist students' learning by design so as to achieve teaching objectives. From the framework of mode choice in the multimodal foreign language teaching, the instructor can understand that the factors of the teaching environment drive the generation of teaching discourse, that is, selecting the teaching generic structure from the genre structure potential of the multiliteracies model, and design teaching practice activities and choose appropriate teaching methods based on the selected teaching generic structure, and select specific modes and mode combinations after determining the teaching methods, and finally carry out teaching activities to achieve teaching objectives.

Following the framework of mode choice, Zhang and Zhang (2014) developed the framework of learning by design for the purpose of cultivating multiliteracies. In the framework, context of culture and context of situation are brought in to control the choice of meaning; learning method is the practical measures for implementing the theory; media and modes are the form and expression for realizing meaning; learning process forms a recursive pattern and meaning is the object of transformation in the learning process, and the multiliteracies are the outcome of the learning process. The transformed meaning and multiliteracies become available design again through the learner's path.

Apart from the theoretical exploration of multimodal and multiliteracies pedagogy, there has been a growing interest in empirical research on its application in teaching practices. It shows the practitioners' enthusiasm in innovating their teaching practices. There are a number of studies on using multimodal pedagogy in language skill instruction. Long and Zhao (2009) trained college students in metacognitive strategies and multimodal listening, and found that the training significantly improved students' English listening performance. In Lv and Mu (2014)'s study, the multimodal pedagogy was introduced into the teaching practice of English reading and the results showed positive effect of the multimodal teaching on college students' reading ability. Other studies further examine multimodal pedagogy's effect on learner psychology. Zeng (2011) conducted a multimodal teaching experiment to explore its efficacy in a video-aural-oral course. The results proved multimodal teaching effective in improving students' listening and speaking skills as well as their autonomy to do listening tasks, and students' attitudes toward English study were shown to be improved. Liu et al. (2013) conducted multimodal teaching experiment and found positive effect of

EFL teachers' multimodal discourse on students' motivation and English performance. Rui and Ji (2017) found that multimodal teaching was an effective way to relieve English speaking anxiety, thus reducing classroom reticence and improving classroom interaction. As PowerPoint (PPT) slides are the most widely used multimodal teaching tool in the classroom, Zhang (2010) investigated the effect of multimodal PPT presentation and found it could improve students' short-term English performance but had limited effect on long-term performance. In another study, Zhang (2013) found that multimodal PPT-based teaching could positively change the students' learning attitudes. Li and Feng (2017) used the genre theory to analyze PPT slides of Linguistic courses and found that teacher-centered knowledge transmission was embodied in the slides. Thus, they proposed PPT design based on multiliteracy pedagogy in order to help teachers design better PPT courseware.

The current age has seen a tremendous impact of modern technology on education with the wide use of audio-visual aids, online platforms and mobile applications. As L2 learners are exposed to more resources for language learning, they need to improve their ability to perceive and produce information of different types of modes. As a result, multimodal pedagogy has been increasingly adopted in the foreign language classroom. Teachers should guide students to make meaning using "Available Designs-Designing-The Redesigned" framework. To meet this objective, teachers need to enhance their awareness of the multiliteracy teaching objective and improve their ability to conduct multimodal teaching informed by multimodal theories. In addition, their skills of using multimedia are essential in achieving the objectives of multimodal and multiliteracy pedagogy. Importantly, teachers need to transform from the traditional central role in the classroom to the supporter of students who are the true center of teaching and learning. They can design teaching, provide resources, offer guidance and encouragement, and help manage and evaluate students' learning. In conclusion, multimodal foreign language teaching has received much attention and exploration, but there is still room for its further theoretical and practical development in China.

Chapter Five Innovation in Technology-enhanced Foreign Language Teaching

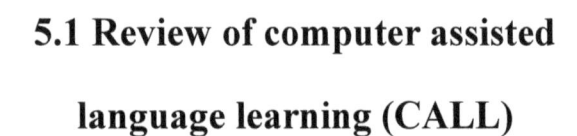

5.1 Review of computer assisted language learning (CALL)

For decades, there has been an imperative to integrate technology into language pedagogy. Computer assisted language learning (CALL) has emerged as an important subfield, linking applied linguistics and educational technology. CALL has developed along with the advancement of technologies, requiring corresponding theoretical development. It's pointed out that much of the CALL research has been theoretically grounded in

SLA theories and approaches, such as usage-based approach, the interaction approach, Skill Acquisition Theory, Sociocultural Theory (Chun, 2016). These theories and approaches emphasize the importance of input and exposure to the linguistic environment. Chun (2016) categorizes the four periods of CALL, each influenced by a dominant theory and accompanied by specific technological devices (see Table 1).

Table 1. Developmental Stages of CALL

Stage	1970s-1980s: Structural CALL	1980s-1990s: Communicative CALL	2000s Integrative CALL	2010s Ecological CALL
Technology	Mainframe	PCs	Multimedia and Internet	Mobile and wearable devices
English teaching paradigm	Grammar translation and audiolingual	Communicative language teaching	Content-based, English for Specific Purposes/English for Academic Purposes	Digital literacies, multiliteracies
View of language	Structural (a formal structural system)	Cognitive (a mentally constructed system)	Sociocognitive (developed in social interaction)	Symbolic and intercultural competence
Principal use of computers	Drill and practice	Communicative exercises	Authentic discourse	Global communication
Principal objective	Accuracy	Fluency	Agency	Identity as global citizens

It's noticeable that the current stage of CALL is termed ecological CALL, reflecting ecological perspectives of SLA. As technologies (mobile and wearable devices) can be assessed anytime and anywhere, language acquisition goes beyond classroom walls. The goal of language teaching and learning also goes beyond the traditional definitions of literacy and directs toward digital literacies and multiliteracies. The scope of language learning is extended beyond communicative competence to symbolic competence, which is "the ability not only to approximate or appropriate for oneself someone else's language, but to shape the very context in which the language is learned and used" (Kramsch, 2011, p. 364). It's essential for L2 learners of the 21st century to acquire cultural know-how to make connections between forms, contexts and meaning in a variety of mediums. Chun (2016) suggests that technology has been fully integrated into second language teaching and learning, in other words, "normalization for CALL". The question facing CALL researchers is not whether technology-based instruction is effective but under what conditions and for whom.

5.2 Technology-enhanced language teaching in China

5.2.1 Reform of English teaching: Integration of technologies

In China, Chen Jianlin (2006) conducted an ecological investigation on the integration of technologies into English teaching and learning in higher education. A new mode of foreign language teaching incorporating computer technology began to emerge as the Ministry of Education called for college English course reforms to address the pressing problem of teacher centeredness and low efficiency of foreign language education. The investigation of courses implementing the new teaching mode found that the use of technology was not transformative and the nature and structure of classroom teaching remained the same, because it was used as an assisting tool to maintain the old structure. Through the analysis of the role of technology in the ecological system of human society, the author argued that the key to the success of the new mode was whether computer technology was treated as an assisting tool or an essential part of the course, and for the teaching structure to transform, the comprehensive integration of computer technology into foreign language courses is imperative.

Subsequent researchers probe into theoretical construction and pedagogical practice of integrating technologies into foreign language teaching. He (2007) proposed an integrative framework in which information technology interacts with the teacher, students and teaching content in the foreign language teaching system. The integrative framework takes constructivism as the learning theory which emphasizes the active role of the learner in acquiring knowledge by constructing meaning with the aid of people and resources. The author further elaborated the foreign language teaching and learning mode integrating information technology. The main objective of the mode is to provide multimodal resources that can activate students' multi-sensory learning and to provide platforms and tools that can facilitate interactive and cooperative learning. Li (2008) had a theoretical discussion of the construction of College English network context. The network context is considered important for web-based language teaching and practice. Its construction relies on various supporting technologies, such as multimedia network platforms, hyper media, virtual reality technology, multimedia communication network technology and artificial intelligence technology. For example, multimedia network platforms facilitate the construction of macro network context that provides massive learning resources, opportunities for interactive, cooperative and autonomous learning.

5.2.2 Internet-based foreign language teaching research

Researching technology and second language teaching and learning has attracted wide attention. Some of the handbooks on SLA and technology (Ziegler & González-Lloret, 2022; Chapelle & Sauro, 2017) have pointed out the directions of researching technology-mediated language teaching, such as theoretical frameworks, research methods, technology for developing specific skills, digital spaces for learning, technology and learner individual differences. In China, Zhang and Liu (2007) put forward a framework for the research of Internet-based foreign language teaching, hoping to guide the research and evaluation of teaching in this field. See Figure 2.

```
┌─────────────────────────────────────────┐
│ Internet-based teaching systematic design│
│ Internet-based speaking teaching;        │
│ Internet-based listening teaching;       │
│ Internet-based reading teaching;         │
│ Internet-based writing teaching;         │
│ Internet-based translation teaching      │
└─────────────────────────────────────────┘
                    ↕
┌─────────────────────────────────────────┐
│ Internet-based teaching factors research │
│ Learning environment research; Learner   │
│ research; Teacher research; Teaching mode│
│ research; Interaction and feedback       │
│ research; assessment research            │
└─────────────────────────────────────────┘
                    ↕
┌─────────────────────────────────────────┐
│ Internet-based teaching theories research│
│ Constructivism; Task-based learning;     │
│ content-based instruction; project-based │
│ learning; autonomous and independent     │
│ learning; cooperative and collaborative  │
│ learning                                 │
└─────────────────────────────────────────┘
```

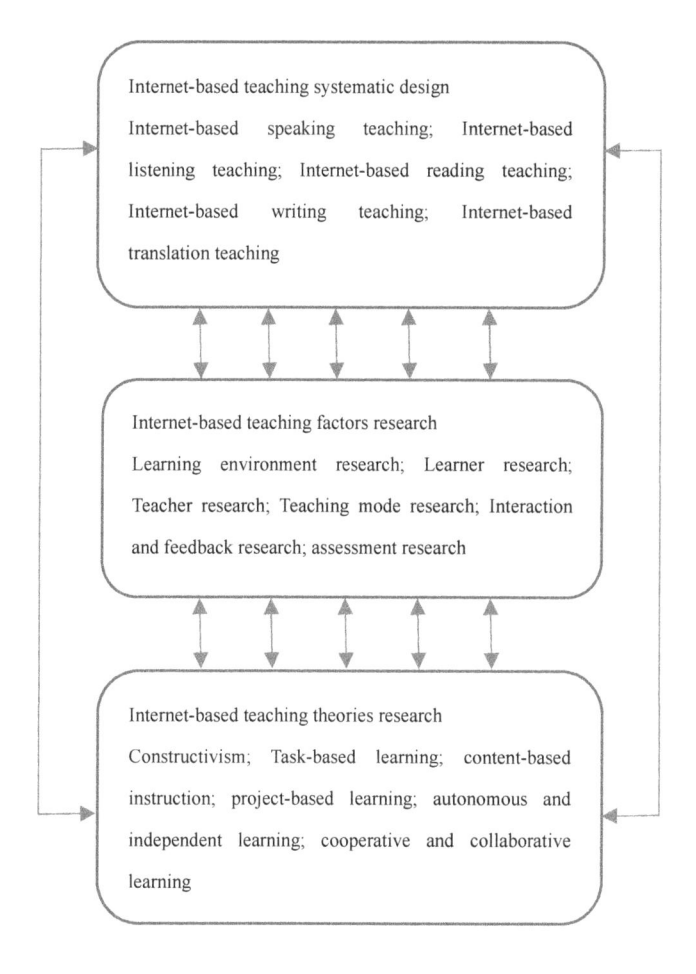

Figure 2. Framework of Internet-based foreign language teaching research

Internet-based teaching theories are those that support and guide Internet-based foreign language teaching research. First, constructivism has had a profound impact on education. Some of its key words include situation, collaboration, communication and construction. Constructivists believe that the learner is the cognitive subject who can accomplish meaning construction in an appropriate situation through collaboration and communication with peers. Second, task-based, content-based and project-based learning theories emphasize student-centeredness and learning by doing. Linking language learning with specific projects, tasks and content, these theories are foundational for researching Internet-based teaching. Third, learner autonomy is essential to Internet-based learning in that learners need to monitor, regulate and evaluate their learning process and outcome. Therefore, autonomous learning theories provide support for Internet-based teaching research.

Factors that are closely related to Internet-based teaching are learning environment, learners and teachers, teaching modes, interaction and feedback, assessment, etc. First, the Internet-based learning environment includes physical and non-physical ones. The former refers to Internet-based teaching platforms and the latter refers to the teaching activities, strategies, interpersonal relationships, etc. Second, language learners have been widely researched in the traditional learning environment, but in the Internet-based learning environment, learners will have very different learning experience, thus demonstrating noticeable individual differences. Likewise, teachers also experience transformations in the Internet-based teaching environment. The roles of teachers and teacher education are the most studied area and are worth further exploration in the face of advancing technologies. Third, Internet-based teaching mode is a hot topic and has arrived at some findings. Future research can be directed toward practice-based theorization. Fourth,

Internet-based teaching and learning provides more ways of interaction such as learner-technology interaction and computer mediated communication, enriching the traditional modes of human-to-human interaction. Finally, assessment of Internet-based teaching includes learner assessment, teacher assessment, assessment of teaching system and learning resources.

Internet-based teaching systematic design research has its basis on relevant theories and practice. The design covers speaking, listening, reading, writing, translating courses or integrated courses. Researching Internet-based teaching design focuses on characteristics of Internet-based courses and how to address problems encountered in these courses.

5.2.3 Research on technology-enhanced foreign language teaching

To better understand the effect of technology on foreign language teaching and learning, researchers have conducted relevant studies over the last 20 years or so. There are a number of empirical studies on learner autonomy in Internet-based learning. Learner autonomy has been an important concept in L2 teaching and learning, and has been widely researched in SLA. Therefore, the research on Internet-based teaching cannot ignore learner autonomy. Chen et al. (2005) conducted Internet-based teaching that aimed at cultivating learner autonomy and explored the effect of this new mode of language teaching. It was found that the students demonstrated great learning potential – good completion of learning tasks and improved autonomous learning ability, showing advantage of the teaching mode. Chen and Xu (2006) investigated a case of college English teaching reform where learner autonomy was the teaching aim and found that autonomous learning was superior to traditional classroom teaching in that it brought about more positive learning attitudes and more intensive language training among the students. Qu and Lv (2016) constructed a teaching model that aimed at fostering learner autonomy in the network environment among English-major students and implemented the teaching model to verify its effect. The authors argue that learner autonomy has both independence and interdependence as its components. Interdependence is indispensable as it represents the social characteristic of learner autonomy. The teaching experiment of the model found that students' metacognition, motivation and learning behavior were significantly improved, showing stronger learner autonomy. Luo (2017) investigated 6

Chinese and American MOOC plats and identified problems existing in online autonomous learning: weak awareness of autonomous learning, limited interaction among learners, insufficient effective language output and imbalanced autonomous learning abilities. To address these problems, the author proposed an autonomous foreign language online learning mode, incorporating interactive online learning environment, comprehensive autonomous learning qualities, and output-driven autonomous learning processes.

Research on L2 teachers' ability to integrate technology in teaching is significant to the field of Internet-based foreign language teaching. By investigating college English teachers' capability of integrating information technology in education, Yang and Liu (2006) discussed the training of L2 teachers in using it in their teaching with its focus on improving teachers' awareness of integrating technology in teaching, basic knowledge of information technology and theories of modern education, operating skills of information technology, as well as skills of integrating information technology in language teaching. Cai and Wu (2014) summarize the operating skills of information technology required of L2 teachers.

Table 3. Operating skills of information technology needed by L2 teachers

Category	Basic	Standard	Advanced
Word processing	Typesetting, table making	Picture making, text inputting	Database making
Excel processing	Student profile analysis, test score analysis	Graph making, dynamic graphs	Database making
Courseware making	PowerPoint layout; font selection	Automation customization	Dubbing
Graphic processing	Downloading online pictures; editing pictures	image stitching, text inputting	dynamic graphs
Information storage	Compressed file storage, PDF storage	hypertext storage	Storage format conversion

Information transmission	Emails; attachments	Group messages	Mail classification
Audio processing	Recording sound; downloading sound	Editing sound; dubbing	Format conversion, removing noise
Video processing	Reading video files from discs; downloading online videos	Editing videos; dubbing	Filming videos

The skills in Table 3 are particularly essential to foreign language teachers as the related technologies can address the needs in foreign language learning such as decomposing, highlighting, repeating, imitating, practicing difficult points and key items. Thus, the comprehensive use of these skills can form a micro teaching system.

5.3 Technology-enhanced teaching modes

MOOCs

In the Information Age, the rise of MOOCs has created more opportunities for traditional classrooms to integrate technology and achieve better teaching effect. MOOC platforms, such as Coursera, Udacity, and edX, offer free online courses from prestigious universities in the U.S. and around the world, which have obvious advantages: low cost, easy access, and high flexibility. Both teachers and students can make use of these platforms to gain excellent resources and explore news forms of learning.

As the trend of technological development, Big Data has triggered the emergence of Massive Open Online Courses (MOOCs), bringing about both challenges to and opportunities for the foreign language teaching in China. Chen (2014) compares MOOCs with traditional class mode in terms of class size, length, motivation, time and place, course design, presentation and evaluation, etc. See Table 4.

Table 4. MOOCs vs. Traditional Class Mode

Dimension	MOOCs	Traditional class
Class size	Not limited, often in thousands	Tens to hundreds
Class length	Micro lecture, around 10 mins	45 mins
Learning motivation	Needs- and interest-oriented	Obligatory
Time and place	Anytime & anywhere	Restricted by time and space
Learning mode	Student-centered, active learning	Teacher-driven, passive learning
Interaction mode	Multidimensional, multifaceted interaction	Face-face communication
Course design	Exquisite	Lacking in creativity
Course presentation	Short videos for unlimited viewing	One off Instruction by the teacher
Course evaluation	Machine, peer and teacher evaluation	Mainly teacher evaluation

MOOCs are fundamentally different from

traditional class mode in every dimension, and can be considered superior in most dimensions as means of foreign language teaching mode. They are more cost-effective and convenient that can cope with pressure of limited teaching resources.

Chen (2015) argues that MOOCs provide teachers with different sets of data from traditional class mode. In the traditional class, teachers are mostly concerned about data related to the subject matter, which are not usually abundant in amount. However, MOOCs can provide tons of data about learning that are previously difficult to notice. The big data produced by MOOCs are conducive to enhancing foreign language teaching. Firstly, personalized learning is made possible by making use of data on the complicated learning activities that tell much about the learners and their diverse needs. Thus, learning resources and methods can be customized. The data also reveal the learning process that can by analyzed to optimize learning effect and efficiency. Secondly, student-centeredness is fully implemented in MOOCs where learners need to take responsibility for their learning, thus cultivating learner autonomy. Thirdly, MOOCs facilitate the creation of other types of teaching mode, such as flipped classroom or blended learning, which are deemed more effective than pure MOOCs. Suitable MOOCs can be selected to complement offline courses so as to achieve high efficiency and better effect. Lastly, MOOCs contribute to teacher professional development. Foreign language teachers are confronted with challenges of mastering information technology and educational technology to better meet the requirements of teachers in the age of big data. Big data produced by MOOCs help teachers to understand, organize, monitor and even research teaching and learning.

MOOC-based teaching has been a hot research topic in China in the recent years. Wang (2014) point outs the future direction of higher education is MOOCs plus classroom sessions, and suggests feasible ways to integrate MOOCs with college English courses through flipped classroom. As college English transits from general English to English for specific purposes (ESP) or general academic English, one problem confronting the transition is the knowledge structure of college English teachers. The teachers don't usually possess adequate subject knowledge to carry out content-based instruction (CBI) required by academic English courses. Meanwhile, the advent of MOOCs, mostly in English, provide learners with wonderful opportunities for learning necessary subject matter knowledge. However, for English learners, language barriers may hinder their learning of MOOCs significantly if they have to engage in self-directed learning. The integration of MOOCs with college English courses can address both problems and enhance the overall learning effect of college English learners. Wang et. al. (2015) constructed the MCE model that incorporated MOOC, CBI and ESP for college English courses. They claim that the teaching model is neither language-driven nor content-driven, but strives for a balance between the two. In the teaching experiment, the experiment group was taught with MCE while the control group was taught with a traditional model that focused on imparting language knowledge and training language skills. It was found that students in the experiment group were much more motivated for English learning than those in the control group because they realized how English learning could facilitate their learning of disciplinary knowledge presented in MOOCs. The experiment group students also outdid the control group students in terms of English performance and learning strategies after one semester, showing the effectiveness of the MCE model.

MOOCs-based teaching is often implemented in some new teaching modes such as flipped classroom and blended learning. In the next section, we will talk about the flipped classroom mode for college English teaching.

Flipped Classroom

Integrated with technology-enhanced learning, such as MOOCs, the flipped classroom is expected to bring positive changes to foreign language teaching and learning.

The flipped classroom is said to be a disruptive innovation that is going to fundamentally change the traditional classroom. Flipped classroom derives from the notion of "inverting the classroom" proposed by Lage, Platt, and Treglia in 2000. By "inverting the classroom", they mean "events that have traditionally taken place inside the classroom now take place outside the classroom and vice versa" (Lage, Platt, & Treglia, 2000, p. 32). In practice, students preview (online) learning materials in advance of class and teachers spend class time working with students to solve learning problems and promote collaborative learning. The flipped classroom teaching approach used by Woodland Park High School teachers Jonathon Bergmann and Aaron Sams proves to be effective in enhancing teaching quality. It's acknowledged that the flipped classroom can promote autonomous learning with online materials and student-centered instruction in the classroom. With convenient access to technology-enhanced learning materials, the flipped classroom mode when appropriately adopted can support classroom teaching and enhance the quality of formal education at different levels.

Researchers and practitioners in China are attentive to the development of flipped class and conducted theoretical research and pedagogical practice. Deng (2016) reviewed studies on the application of flipped classroom in college English teaching, and identified the process of the teaching mode: 1) analyzing learner factors; 2) developing teaching resources; 3) designing teaching procedure; 4) regulating learning process. He also summarized the task characteristics of this teaching mode. The tasks are student-centered, supported by technology, and require independent and collaborative learning. They also enable personalized learning. Hu and Wu (2014) reported the findings of a teaching experiment involving flipped classroom. In the college English course, the teacher made videos and developed online tests for students to learn on their own before class, followed by class sessions where project-based learning was implemented. Students worked with peers on a project that involved group oral presentation and individual writing, under the guidance of the teacher. Surveys reflected students' overall satisfaction with the MOOC-based flipped classroom model. There were reasons for the satisfaction. The use of MOOC enhanced learning because students were able to study at their own pace, thus meeting their learning and emotional needs. Also, the flipped classroom afforded more opportunities for students to communicate and collaborate with teachers and peers and enabled them to improve language knowledge and skills significantly.

Researchers have also studied how the flipped classroom influences the way teachers teach and students learn. Cheng (2014) argued that teachers no longer serve as the provider of knowledge as students have easy access to knowledge in the information age. A new paradigm needs to be established in foreign language teaching where teachers provide constructive learning service to students. That is to say, they become guides, organizers, facilitators and evaluators of learning so that students can achieve the optimal learning results by making use of new technology. Role-changing of teachers directly impacts how students learn. Under the guidance and support of teachers, students need to cultivate autonomous learning ability and collaborative learning ability. Lv (2016) constructed the flipped classroom based autonomous learning mode which was applied in college English teaching. It was found that the mode was effective in enhancing the students' comprehensive English proficiency, fostering their autonomous learning ability and improving their attitudes towards learning English.

The tasks and activities used in the mode of flipped classroom are important for achieving the desired effect of language teaching. In the discussion of constructing a flipped classroom model for college English education, Qu (2017) illustrates how the different tasks and activities in the flipped classroom mode can meet Bloom's educational objectives. See Figure 3.

Educational objectives		Flipped classroom approaches
↑	Creating	While-class and post-class creative work
	Evaluating	While-class and post-class evaluations and critiques
	Analyzing	While-class and post-class discussions
	Applying	While-class or post-class problem-solving tasks
	Understanding	Pre-class quizzes and while-class teacher-support
	Remembering	Pre-class self-study through video lessons

Figure 3. Educational Objectives of the Flipped Classroom Mode

The tasks and activities are not new to foreign language teaching. But without the flipped classroom concept, they may not be arranged in a systematic way that can achieve effective educational objectives and foreign language learning objectives.

5.4 Artificial intelligence and foreign language teaching

The recent technological development has brought artificial intelligence (AI) to language teaching and AI-driven language teaching and learning is expected to be widely accepted in the post-pandemic era. Handley (2024) points out that language educators need a more in-depth understanding of AI and how it works. When discussing whether AI can replace the language teacher, she argues that a good language teacher requires not only a distinctive form of pedagogical knowledge but also particularly strong interpersonal skills, which are not adequately demonstrated by current AI. It's pointed out that some of the popular AI-powered tools have limitations in terms of the effectiveness of delivering instruction and facilitating learning. Also, AI's excessive feedback on form rather than content may have a demotivating effect. Therefore, the conclusion is that current AI at best can complement human teachers to "to engage with knowledge and meaning, provide more creative opportunities to use language, and engage with the whole learner at a human level" (p. 553).

Chinese scholars have explored the application of AI in foreign language teaching. In 2006, Jia presented an innovative intelligent web-based English tutoring system, CSIEC, which was said to overcome the disadvantages of existing CALL systems and fulfill the actual demands of English teaching and learning in China. The intelligent tutoring system has a number of unique functions. For example, users can have real time chat with the system at any time without restrictions on the chat content and duration. Also, the system can detect the user's spelling and grammar errors and prompt the user to correct errors instead of pointing out the errors. It's worth noticing that the system supports simultaneous chatting of multiple users, thus creating a human-machine context to facilitate distant language learning. Hong (2018) constructed an ecological teaching mode of college English involving the use of AI. On the one hand, AI can access all sorts of learner data such as basic information, learning profile, and then complete learner modelling with the aim of supporting personalized learning. On the other hand, AI enables personalized teaching, affords virtual learning environment and realizes automatic learning management. The author argues that AI will play an active role in analyzing learner differences, providing learners with tailored learning materials, and conducting dynamic and formative assessment of the learning process. Also, AI's strong data processing function can analyze and evaluate the learning effect, provide learners with targeted feedback and intervention, thus facilitating ecological teaching of college English. Zhang and Hong (2023) explain how conversational AI technologies such as ChatGPT enable the intrinsic mechanism of foreign language learning by focusing on self-directed learning and role-changing of teachers. For learners, ChatGPT enables personalized learning, exploratory learning, and provides diversified learning activities and customized learning plans. For teachers, ChatGPT enables them to design and prepare teaching more efficiently and to assess students' learning outcomes more effectively. As AI takes over some roles of teachers, such as need analyst, conversation partner, feedback provider, learning evaluator, teachers need to focus more on designing, facilitating and monitoring learning. It's suggested that teachers should help learners to better regulate their feelings and emotions in the process of learning. The authors also discuss the strategies of using ChatGPT to develop students' critical thinking ability. Unlike traditional teaching mode that emphasizes skill training and proficiency assessment, AI-enhanced foreign language teaching should stress the cultivation of learners' critical and creative thinking, and develop multiple methods to assess learning achievements.

While the potential value of AI as a tool for foreign language teaching and learning has been widely acknowledged, empirical research is in urgent need to evaluate AI's effectiveness in facilitating the achievement of various goals in foreign language education.

5.5 Corpus-based language teaching and learning

Corpus linguistics has been a promising field of research in recent years. Corpus linguistics makes extensive use of computers for analysis to deal with machine-readable texts as the basis on which to study specific research questions. Many would agree that corpus linguistics is not only about collecting and analyzing language data, but also a discipline in and of itself. The development of the field has gone hand in hand with the advancement of modern technology. This field heavily relies on language resources, and some corpora have been shared for free or for low cost, and others can be accessed online for concordance service.

A group of Chinese scholars (Shi et.al., 2010) coauthored an article on the topic of corpus linguistics and foreign language teaching in China. The article points out the role of corpus linguistics as resource and tool provider as well as theoretical and pedagogical guidance for foreign language teaching. As resources for teaching, language facts from corpora are particularly suitable for teaching and can even be compiled into textbooks. The use of corpus linguistics can effectively solve the problem of lacking authentic materials, thus improving teaching and learning efficiency. It's also argued that not only language data but also non-linguistic knowledge can be extracted from corpora. To this end, researchers and practitioners need to possess the capability of text data mining, and the ability to turn data into knowledge. When discussing the application of corpus linguistics in foreign language teaching, the article mentions a number of areas that should be noticed. First, it's necessary to build learner corpora, where characteristics of language errors can be identified, so that the teacher can specifically address learning difficulties and train learning strategies. Second, it's suggested that research findings of corpus linguistics that concern formulaic expressions, word collocations and error analysis be complied as corpora so that teachers can make use of them to design teaching more effectively. Third, data-driven learning can be promoted among advanced learners who will observe and analyze language facts, synthesize and induce language rules under the guidance of the teacher. Given that learners may be "lost" in massive language facts, corpus tools such as concordancor that facilitate data-driven learning can be utilized.

Instead of being regarded merely as providing resources and tools, corpus linguistics has been increasingly recognized as being able to afford new perspectives, new concepts and new methods to the field of linguistics, which in turn has impacted applied linguistics. Theoretical findings of corpus linguistics are believed to contribute to foreign language teaching, for instance, "lexicogrammar", "spoken grammar", "phraseology", etc. The findings make practitioners reflect on their practices. Should grammar and vocabulary be taught separately? Should vocabulary teaching focus on words or phrases? Should the teaching of collocations focus on their forms or meanings? There's no doubt that application of corpus linguistics can revolutionize language teaching, by changing the ways we approach such areas of pedagogy as curriculum design, materials development, teaching methodology and teacher training.

While many applied linguists and practitioners have realized the value and potential of corpus linguistics and attempted to verify the theoretical effectiveness through teaching practices, corpus-assisted language teaching has not yet become a mainstream pedagogy, for a number of reasons: 1) teachers are not usually adequately trained to build and use corpora, and language; 2) teachers find it very time-consuming to build corpora and train students in their use; 3) language classrooms may not be well-equipped to incorporate corpus technology instruction. Above all, there seems to exist a gap between corpus linguistics and language teaching that needs to be bridged, that is, the gap between teaching implications in corpus linguistics literature and concerns of language teaching practitioners. To bridge this gap, corpus linguistics findings need to be interpreted and used together with research findings of foreign language teaching and second language acquisition.

Chapter Six Innovation in Project-Based Language Learning

6.1 Review of project-based language learning

Project-based learning (PBL) is a comprehensive teaching approach that guides learners to be engaged in a string of inquiry activities and complete the final product (Blumenfeld et al., 1991). Learners are put in an environment where they can cooperate with peers to solve a problem and also acquire knowledge. Project-based language learning (PBLL), as a pedagogical strategy for second language acquisition, emphasizes student participation and engagement through collaborative problem-solving while using the target language

(Beckett & Slater, 2019). As a result, PBLL can help students to acquire knowledge and skills of the target language and also develop non-linguistic skills, such as collaborative learning ability and critical thinking ability.

PBL has its theoretical foundation in constructivism which holds that learners acquire knowledge based on prior experience and PBL provides learners with opportunities to make meaning connection between new knowledge and prior experience. PBL advocates solving real-world problems and using authentic materials, and the interaction and cooperation in a group provides authentic and meaningful learning experience. Social constructivism, a branch of constructivism, can explain why PBL works. Vygotsky's zone of proximal distance (ZPD) refers to the distance between the learner's actual development and potential development. The former is represented by the learner's ability developed from self-directed learning, and the latter reflects a learner's ability developed with the scaffolding of an instructor or other more capable learners. ZPD can be created by PBL where students of different levels are grouped together to scaffold each other through cooperative interaction (Sidman-Taveau & Milner-Bolotin, 2001).

Scholars (Beckett & Slater, 2005; Stroller, 2006) have attempted to construct the PBL operational framework. For example, Beckett & Slater (2005) proposed "the project framework", a methodological tool, which would "help teachers to raise their students' awareness of how language and skills develop through projects at the same time as content is learned" (p. 109). In a word, the project framework addresses the simultaneous learning of language, content, and skills. It contains two major components: the planning graphic and the project diary. The graphic is directed toward the categorization of the target language, content, and skills. The project diary provides a weekly summarization task that encourages students to make explicit the language, content and skills they have been using during the week. The authors explored the implementation of the project framework through empirical research and found that all the subjects were able to use the project framework including the planning graphic and the project diary as a tool to accomplish their learning goals in terms of language, content and skills.

In the past decades, PBLL has gained popularity in many EFL countries as a means of providing opportunities for language learners to use authentic language (Poonpon, 2017). Studies of PBLL focus on the pedagogical practices and its effect on learners' skill acquisition. Fried-Booth (1982) carried out PBLL where English learners were required to create a city guidebook for disabled tourists, which is regarded as a classic project that integrate learning and doing.

Subsequently, researchers from both English speaking and non-English speaking countries followed suit and reported teaching practices of PBLL. The research findings show great potential of PBLL in foreign language teaching and learning. Recently, PBLL has been used in many EFL classrooms to enhance learners' motivation and creativity (Shin, 2018). Recent studies have also attempted to integrate PBL into specific English courses, such as academic writing and English literature. Moreover, the integration of technology into PBLL has proven to enhance learning via the creation of "real-world digital contexts" (Beckett, Slater, & Mohan, 2020, p. 220). PBLL in a digital context is endorsed by language learners due to its practicality and high efficiency (Knoblauch, 2022). EFL teachers in different contexts perceive technology-assisted PBLL as a desired teaching approach although they admit there are challenges in the process of implementation (Garib, 2022).

Other research of technology-assisted PBLL concerns solving authentic problems through virtual reality classrooms (Sidman-Taveau & Milner-Bolotin, 2001; Morales, Bang, & Andre, 2013), and PBLL with social messaging applications such as WhatsApp or Facebook (Avci & Adiguzel, 2017).

6.2 Localization of PBLL in China

Chinese scholar Zhang Wenzhong has focused on researching PBLL in foreign language teaching in China. Acknowledging the potential of PBLL in improving foreign language teaching, Zhang carried out several PBLL teaching experiments and summarized his views on localizing PBLL in China. PBLL and skill-oriented English teaching have very different teaching objectives in that PBLL essentially is student-centered and creativity-oriented (Zhang, 2012), which is more compatible with the current foreign language teaching reform goals. Based on his six-year PBL pedagogical practice, Zhang (2015) localized PBL and proposed an innovation-oriented project-based learning mode (*i*PBL), which aims to promote critical thinking and innovative ability in English majors. The research-based *i*PBL model orients itself to innovative ability cultivation and features six progression stages promoting integrated comprehensive training. See Figure 4.

```
┌─────────────────────────────────┐      ┌─────────────────────────────┐
│ 1. Pre-project stage:           │─────▶│ Project learning enthusiasm │
│    Orientation of the course    │      │                             │
│    and PBL                      │      │                             │
└─────────────────────────────────┘      └─────────────────────────────┘
                │                                       │
                ▼                                       ▼
┌─────────────────────────────────┐      ┌─────────────────────────────┐
│ 2. Project preparation and      │─────▶│ Driving questions, learning │
│    launching stage: Grouping    │      │ contract                    │
│    and topic selection          │      │                             │
└─────────────────────────────────┘      └─────────────────────────────┘
                │                                       │
                ▼                                       ▼
┌─────────────────────────────────┐      ┌─────────────────────────────┐
│ 3. Project designing stage:     │─────▶│ Project research proposal   │
│    Designing research plan and  │      │                             │
│    procedure, determining       │      │                             │
│    research tools               │      │                             │
└─────────────────────────────────┘      └─────────────────────────────┘
                │                                       │
                ▼                                       ▼
┌─────────────────────────────────┐      ┌─────────────────────────────┐
│ 4. Project implementing stage:  │─────▶│ Project interim results,    │
│    Collecting and analyzing     │      │ research report draft       │
│    data, writing project report │      │                             │
└─────────────────────────────────┘      └─────────────────────────────┘
                │                                       │
                ▼                                       ▼
┌─────────────────────────────────┐      ┌─────────────────────────────┐
│ 5. Project presenting stage:    │─────▶│ Project results/paper       │
│    Presenting project results   │      │ presentation                │
│    with guidance, followed by   │      │                             │
│    feedback                     │      │                             │
└─────────────────────────────────┘      └─────────────────────────────┘
                │                                       │
                ▼                                       ▼
┌─────────────────────────────────┐      ┌─────────────────────────────┐
│ 6. Post-project stage:          │─────▶│ Reflection, report          │
│    Compiling project results,   │      │ collection, grading         │
│    reflecting on learning, and  │      │                             │
│    evaluating the course        │      │                             │
└─────────────────────────────────┘      └─────────────────────────────┘
```

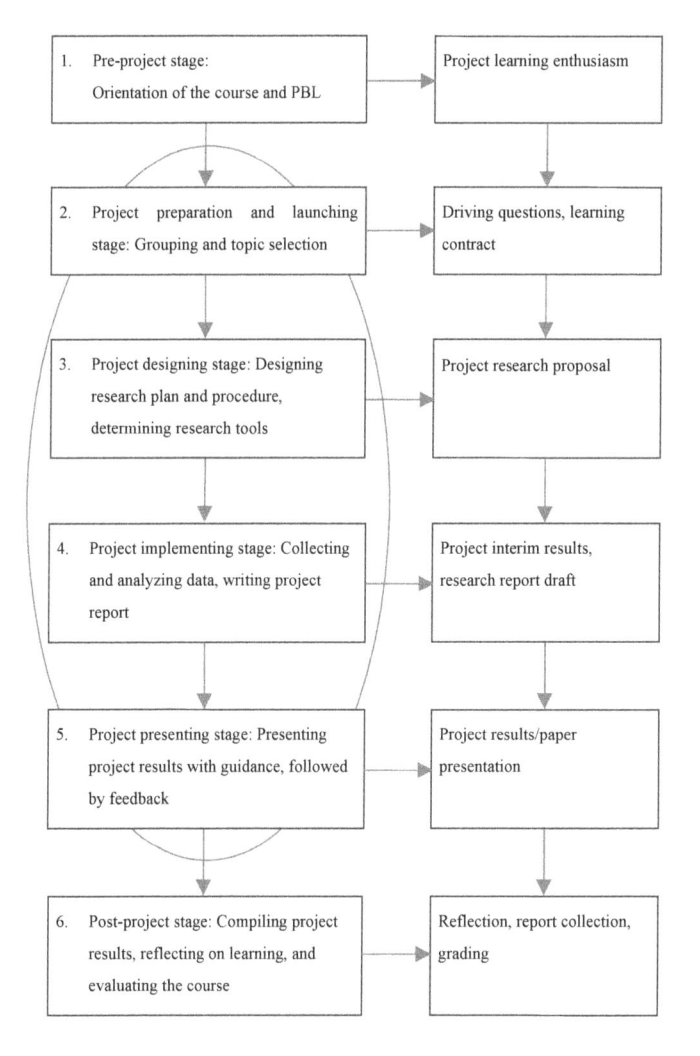

Figure 4. *i*PBL Teaching Model

The tasks and activities in the *i*PBL teaching model are as follows. At the pre-project stage, teachers can introduce the concept of PBL and its advantages in English learning, as well as requirements of the project as part of the course evaluation. Students are invited to talk about their needs and interests so as to choose project topics that can better meet their needs and interests. At the project preparation and launching stage, teachers guide groups of students to choose project topics and raise research questions. Teachers and students should also sign learning contracts to ensure that everyone takes due responsibility in PBL. At the project designing stage, teachers should provide theoretical guidance and help students determine research scope, focus and feasibility. Also, they should guide students to design research including research procedure and tools. Students need to work in groups to complete the research proposals and present them in front of the class. At the project implementing stage, teachers need to focus their teaching on methods of data collection and analysis, and paper writing. Students should submit their interim results and draft of paper for guidance on further improvement. At the project presenting stage, teachers should provide students with support on language skills and presentation skills, and students need to prepare for the presentation by putting together project results and doing rehearsals. At the post-project stage, teachers need to evaluate students' performance and students should reflect on the learning process and results as well as achievements and problems, under the guidance of the teacher. The six stages constitute a PBL teaching procedure that aims to train critical thinking and innovative ability of language learners.

Chinese researchers have delved into the application of PBLL in different teaching contexts. Yang and Han (2012) explored the effect of PBL in College English academic writing course and found that the experimental group outperformed the control group in the aspects of thesis selection, investigation procedures and methods, data collection and analysis, writing norms, formats and strategies, etc. The results indicated that the students from the experimental group enhanced their awareness and capabilities in practical, exploratory and creative studies as well as their competence in general and academic English writing. Long (2015) conducted an empirical study based on the design of PBL flipped classroom in College English course, and found the teaching significantly improved students' learning attitude, enhanced their language proficiency and promoted collaborative learning. Through reviewing the literature, Yang and Diao (2022) found that PBLL are effective in enhancing both language learning and content learning, learning motivation, critical thinking, collaborative learning, and cross-culture communication skills. They also found differences in the attitudes of learners and teachers towards PBLL. Some studies show that both learners and teachers acknowledge the positive effects of PBLL while other studies show that learners of different proficiencies adopt different attitudes towards PBLL. The challenges pointed out by learners include the complexity and difficulty of PBLL, time requirement of projects and anxiety about presentations. As to researching PBL, Wang and Wang (2022) analyze the modes of organization and focal areas of work of the Project-based College English Virtual Teaching & Research Center, which is among the first batch of experimental virtual teaching and research centers approved by the Ministry of Education of China. The analysis shows that the center aims to excel at teaching materials development, teaching methodology and pedagogical research through coordinated collaboration among school-based or virtual teaching & research groups, as well as sharing academic and teaching resources, expertise, and pedagogical research achievements.

Despite the proved effectiveness of PBLL –

generally positive learning outcomes and positive perceptions of students and teachers, PBLL remains relatively rare in foreign language teaching practices, as the application of PBLL is challenging for both students and teachers. It will take continuous effort of researchers and practitioners to construct feasible teaching modes to fulfill the promising potential of PBLL.

References

Avci, H., & Adiguzel, T. Project-based foreign language learning in a mobile blended collaborative learning setting: A case study of EFL learners [A]. In P. Resta & S. Smith (Eds.), Association for the advancement of computing in education[C]. Austin, Texas, 2017:740-743.

Atkinson, D., T. Nishino, E. Churchill, and H. Okada. Alignment and interaction in a sociocognitive approach to second language acquisition [J]. The Modern Language Journal, 2007, 91(2): 169–188.

Beckett, G. & Slater, T. Global Perspectives on Project-Based Language Learning, Teaching, and Assessment: Key Approaches, Technology Tools, and Frameworks [M]. New York, NY:

Routledge, 2019.

Beckett, G. H. & Slater, T. The project framework: A tool for language, content, and skills integration [J]. ELT Journal, 2005, 59(2): 108-116.

Beckett, G. H., Slater, T., & Mohan, B. A. Philosophical foundation, theoretical approaches, and gaps in the literature [A]. In G. H. Beckett & T. Slater (Eds.), Global perspectives on project-based language learning, teaching, and assessment: Key approaches, technology tools, and frameworks[C]. New York: Routledge, 2020:3-22.

Blumenfeld, P. C., Soloway, E., Marx, R.W., Krajcik, J.S., Guzdial, M., & Palincsar, A. Motivating project-based learning: Sustaining the doing, supporting the learning [J]. Educational Psychologist, 1991(26): 369-398.

Camiciottoli, C. & Cubillo, C. Introduction: The

nexus of multimodality, multimodal literacy, and English language teaching in research and practice in higher education settings [J]. System, 2018(77):1-9.

Chapelle, C. A. & Sauro, S. (Eds.) The Handbook of Technology and Second Language Teaching and Learning[C]. Hoboken, NJ: John Wiley & Sons, 2017.

Chomsky, N. Aspects of the Theory of Syntax [M]. Cambridge, MA: MIT Press, 1965.

Chun, D. M. The role of technology in SLA research [J]. Language Learning & Technology, 2016, 20(2): 98–115.

Cope, B., & Kalantzis, M. "Multiliteracies": New literacies, new learning [J]. Pedagogies: International Journal, 2009, 4(3): 164–195.

Costa, A., M. J. Pickering, and A. Sorace. Alignment in second language dialogue [J]. Language and Cognitive Processes, 2008, 23(4): 528–556.

Ellis, R. & Shintani, N. Exploring Language Pedagogy through Second Language Acquisition Research [M]. London & New York: Routledge, 2014.

Fried-Booth, D. Project work with advanced classes [J]. ELT journal, 1982, 36(2): 98-103.

Garib A. "Actually, It's Real Work": EFL Teachers' Perceptions of Technology‐Assisted Project‐Based Language Learning in Lebanon, Libya, and Syria [J]. TESOL Quarterly, 2022, 57(4): 1434-1462.

Handley, Z. Has artificial intelligence rendered language teaching obsolete? [J]. The Modern Language Journal, 2024(2): 548 - 555.

Izumi, S. Comprehension and Production Processes in Second Language Learning: In Search of the Psycholinguistic Rationale of the Output Hypothesis [J]. Applied Linguistics, 2003, 24(2):168-196.

Knoblauch, C. Digital project-based learning in the

higher education sector [A]. In Innovations in Learning and Technology for the Workplace and Higher Education, Proceedings of 'the learning ideas conference'[C]. Springer International Publishing, 2022:170-179.

Krahnke K. Approaches to Syllabus Design for Foreign Language Teaching [M]. New York: Prentice Hall, 1987.

Kramsch, C. The symbolic dimensions of the intercultural [J]. Language Teaching, 2011, 44(3): 354–367.

Kress, G. Literacy in the New Media Age [M]. London: Routledge.2003

Kress, G. Multimodality: A Social Semiotic Approach to Contemporary Communication [M]. London: Routledge, 2010.

Liu, J. Visual images interpretive strategies in multimodal texts [J]. Journal of Language Teaching and Research, 2013, 4(6): 1259-1263.

Marsh, D. CLIL/EMILE-The European Dimension: Actions, Trends and Foresight Potential [M]. Brussels: European Commission, 2002.

Morales, T. M., Bang, E., & Andre, T. A one-year case study: Understanding the rich potential of project-based learning in a virtual reality class for high school students [J]. Journal of Science Education and Technology, 2013, 22(5): 91-806.

New London Group. A pedagogy of multiliteracies: Designing social futures [J]. Harvard Educational Review, 1996, 66(1): 60-90.

O'Halloran, K. L., Tan, S., & Smith, B. A. Multimodal approaches to English for academic purposes [A]. In K. Hyland, & P. Shaw (Eds.), The Routledge handbook of English for academic purposes [C]. London & New York: Routledge, 2016: 256-269.

Peng, J., Wang, C., & Lu, X. Effect of the linguistic complexity of the input text on alignment, writing fluency, and writing accuracy in the continuation task [J]. Language Teaching Research, 2020, 24(3): 364-381.

Pickering, M. J. and S. Garrod. Toward a mechanistic psychology of dialogue [J]. Behavioral and Brain Sciences, 2004, 27(2): 169–226.

Poonpon, K. Enhancing English skills through project-based learning [J]. The English Teacher, 2017(40): 1–10.

Qu L. A Study on the Flipped Classroom Model for College English Education [J]. US-China Foreign Language, 2017, 15(9): 577-581.

Royce, T. & Bowcher, W. (Eds.). New Directions in the Analysis of Multimodal Discourse [C]. London: Lawrance Erlbaum Associates, 2007.

Selfe, C. L. (Ed.). Multimodal Composition: Resources for Teachers [C]. Cresskill: Hampton Press, 2007.

Shin, M. Effects of project-based learning on

students' motivation and self-efficacy [J]. English Teaching, 2018, 73(1): 95–113.

Sidman-Taveau, R. & Milner-Bolotin, M. Constructivist inspiration: A project based model for L2 learning in virtual worlds [J]. Texas Papers in Foreign Language, 2001, 6(1): 63-82.

Spada, N. & Lightbown, M. Form-Focused Instruction: Isolated or Integrated? [J]. TESOL Quarterly, 2008, 42(2):181-207.

Stein, P. Rethinking resources: Multimodal pedagogies in the ESL classroom [J]. TESOL Quarterly, 2000, 34: 333–336.

Street, B., Pahl, K., & Rowsell, J. (2011). Multimodality and new literacy studies [A]. In C. Jewitt (Ed.), The Routledge handbook of multimodal analysis [C]. London: Routledge, 2011: 191-200.

Thwaites, T. Multiliteracies: A New Direction for Arts Education [EB/OL]. 1999.

http://www.swin.edu.au/aare/99pap/thw99528.ht.

Walsh, M. Multimodal literacy: What does it mean for classroom practice? [J]. Australian Journal of Language and Literacy, 2010(3): 211-223.

Wang, C. & Wang, M. Effect of alignment on L2 written production [J]. Applied Linguistics, 2015(36): 503-526.

Wen Q. The production-oriented approach to teaching university students English in China [J]. Language Teaching, 2016, 51(4):526-540.

Zhang, S. & Zhang, J. Effects of a xu-argument based iterative continuation task on an EFL learner's linguistic and affective development: Evidence from errors, self-initiated error corrections, and foreign language learning attitude [J]. System, 2021(98):1-12.

Zhang, X. Reading–writing integrated tasks, comprehensive corrective feedback, and EFL writing development [J]. Language Teaching

Research, 2017, 21(2): 217-240.

Ziegler, N. & González-Lloret, M. The Routledge Handbook of Second Language Acquisition and Technology [M]. Abingdon: Routledge, 2022.

蔡龙权,吴维屏. 关于把信息技术作为现代外语教师能力构成的思考[J]. 外语电化教学, 2014(1):45-53.

陈冰冰. MOOCs课程模式:贡献和困境[J]. 外语电化教学, 2014(3):38-43.

陈坚林. 大学英语教学新模式下计算机网络与外语课程的有机整合——对计算机"辅助"外语教学概念的生态学考察[J]. 外语电化教学, 2006(6):3-10.

陈坚林. 大数据时代的慕课与外语教学研究——挑战与机遇[J]. 外语电化教学, 2015(1):3-8+16.

陈美华, 邵争, 郑玉琪. 基于计算机和网络的大学英语自主学习模式研究[J]. 外语电化教学, 2005(6):19-23.

陈青松, 许罗迈. 大学英语教学中的网络化外语自主学习[J]. 外语界, 2006(6):16-23.

程云艳. 直面挑战"翻转"自我——新教育范式下大学外语教师的机遇与挑战[J].外语电化教学, 2014(3):44-47+74.

邓笛. 翻转课堂模式在大学英语教学中的应用研究述评[J]. 外语界, 2016(4):89-96.

邓海龙. "产出导向法"与"任务型教学法"比较: 理念、假设与流程[J]. 外语教学, 2018, 39(03):55-59.

顾曰国. 多媒体、多模态学习剖析[J]. 外语电化教学, 2007(2):3-12.

桂诗春, 冯志伟, 杨惠中, 等. 语料库语言学与中国外语教学[J]. 现代外语, 2010, 33(04):419-426.

何培芬. 网络信息技术与外语课程整合的理论与方法[J]. 外语电化教学, 2007(1):14-19.

胡杰辉, 伍忠杰. 基于MOOC的大学英语翻转课堂教学模式研究[J]. 外语电化教学, 2014(6):40-45.

胡壮麟. 社会符号学研究中的多模态化[J]. 语言教学与研究, 2007(1):1-10.

洪常春. 人工智能时代大学英语生态教学模式构建研究[J]. 外语电化教学, 2018(6):29-34.

洪炜, 石薇. 读后续写任务在汉语二语量词学习中的效应[J]. 现代外语, 2016, 39(06):806-818+873-874.

黄国文. 新文科背景下的外语教育[J]. 语言教育, 2022(4): 3-11.

贾积有. 人工智能技术的远程教育应用探索——"希赛可"智能型网上英语学习系统[J]. 现代教育技术, 2006(2):26-29+21.

姜琳, 陈燕, 詹剑灵. 读后续写中的母语思维研究[J]. 外语与外语教学, 2019(3):8-16+143.

李新民. 大学英语网络语境构建的理论探索[J]. 外语电化教学, 2008(1):9-13.

李燕飞, 冯德正. PPT 课件设计与语言学知识建构: 多元读写教学法视角[J]. 电化教育研究, 2017, 38(05):95-100.

李战子. 多模式话语的社会符号学分析[J]. 外语

研究, 2003(5):1-8+80.

刘丽, 王初明. (2018). "续论"与对外汉语动结式的学习[J]. 广东外语外贸大学学报, 29(03):21-28.

刘秀丽, 张德禄, 张宜波. 外语教师多模态话语与学生学习积极性的关系研究[J].外语电化教学, 2013(3):3-9.

龙菡. 大学英语项目式翻转课堂教学设计及实证研究[J]. 中国教育学刊, 2015(S2):229-230.

龙宇飞, 赵璞. 大学英语听力教学中元认知策略与多模态交互研究[J]. 外语电化教学, 2009(4):58-62+74.

骆蓉. 网络环境下外语自主学习模式研究——基于中美 MOOC 平台调查[J]. 外语界, 2017(6):29-36.

吕美嘉, 牟为姣. 多模态教学模式对大学生英语阅读能力影响的研究[J]. 中国电化教育, 2014(12):129-132.

吕婷婷. 基于翻转课堂的大学英语自主学习模式研究[J]. 中国外语, 2016, 13(01):77-83.

缪海燕. 外语写作互动的语篇协同研究[J]. 现代外语, 2017, 40(05):630-641+730.

缪海燕, 王启. 多轮续写对英语写作的动态影响[J]. 现代外语, 2022, 45(04): 513-525.

彭红英. 英语学习者写作连贯性的实证研究[J]. 解放军外国语学院学报, 2017, 40(04):87-92.

瞿莉莉, 吕乐. 网络环境下英语专业学生自主学习培养模式研究[J]. 外语电化教学, 2016(4):9-14.

芮燕萍, 冀慧君. 多模态听说教学对口语焦虑与课堂沉默的影响[J]. 外语电化教学, 2017(6):50-55.

孙曙光. "师生合作评价"课堂反思性实践研究[J]. 现代外语, 2017, 40(03):397-406+439.

王初明. 以"续"促学[J]. 现代外语, 2016, 39(06):784-793+873.

王初明. 从"以写促学"到"以续促学"[J]. 外语教学与研究, 2017, 49(04):547-556+639-640.

王初明. 如何提高读后续写中的互动强度[J]. 外

语界, 2018(5): 40-45.

王初明. 续论高效促学外语的内在逻辑[J]. 外语界, 2021(6): 2-7.

王海啸, 王文宇. 创新创优共建共享——"项目式大学英语教学模式改革虚拟教研室"建设路径探索[J]. 外语界, 2022(4):8-15.

王敏, 蔡宁. 读后续写输入文本语言复杂度对二语写作中语言发展的影响[J]. 外语教学与研究, 2022, 54(6):890-901+960.

王启, 王初明. 以续促学英语关系从句[J]. 外语教学理论与实践, 2019(3):1-5+18.

王启, 王凤兰. 汉语二语读后续写的协同效应[J]. 现代外语, 2016, 39(06):794-805+873.

王启, 钟丽珍, 王伟权, 杨航, 钟文蓓. 语境再现线索导向对二语读后续写协同效应的影响[J]. 中国外语, 2022,19(4):62-69.

王守宏, 刘金玲, 付文平. "慕课"背景下以内容为依托的大学英语ESP教学模式研究[J]. 中国电化教育, 2015(4):97-101+120.

王欣. MOOC视域中的大学外语教学模式的路径

选择[J]. 黑龙江高教研究, 2014(8):157-159.

文秋芳. 构建"产出导向法"理论体系[J]. 外语教学与研究, 2015, 47(04):547-558+640.

文秋芳. "师生合作评价":"产出导向法"创设的新评价形式[J]. 外语界, 2016(5):37-43.

文秋芳. "产出导向法"的中国特色[J]. 现代外语, 2017, 40(03):348-358+438.

文秋芳. 产出导向法:中国外语教育理论创新探索[M]. 北京:外语教学与研究出版社. 2020.

辛声. 读后续写任务条件对二语语法结构习得的影响[J]. 现代外语, 2017, 40(04):507-517+584.

熊淑慧. 议论文对比续写的协同效应研究[J]. 解放军外国语学院学报, 2018, 41(05):85-92.

徐富平, 王初明. 复诊续写任务促学医学汉语词汇的效应[J]. 解放军外国语学院学报, 2020, 43(01):17-24+159.

杨翠萍, 刘鸣放. 大学英语教师的信息化教育技术能力及其培养[J]. 外语界, 2006(4):57-62.

杨华. 读后续写对中高级水平外语学习者写作修

辞的学习效应研究[J]. 外语教学与研究, 2018, 50(04):596-607+641.

杨莉萍, 韩光. 基于项目式学习模式的大学英语学术写作教学实证研究[J]. 外语界, 2012(5):8-16

杨鲁新, 刁慧莹. 项目式学习在外语教学中的应用研究：回顾与展望[J]. 外语教学, 2024, 45(01):69-75.

曾庆敏. 多模态视听说教学模式对听说能力发展的有效性研究[J]. 解放军外国语学院学报, 2011, 34(06):72-76+128.

詹剑灵, 姜琳, 黄灵灵. 对比续写中的二语写作焦虑研究[J]. 解放军外国语学院学报, 2022, 45(02):61-69+160.

张德禄. 多模态话语理论与媒体技术在外语教学中的应用[J]. 外语教学, 2009, 30(04):15-20.

张德禄. 多模态外语教学的设计与模态调用初探[J]. 中国外语, 2010, 7(03):48-53+75.

张德禄. 多模态学习能力培养模式探索[J]. 外语研究, 2012(2):9-14.

张德禄, 王璐. 多模态话语模态的协同及在外语教学中的体现[J]. 外语学刊, 2010(2):97-102.

张红玲, 刘云波. 从网络外语教学研究现状看网络外语教学研究的学科框架[J].外语电化教学, 2007(4):8-13.

张琳, 秦婷. 读后续写对英语专业学生写作焦虑和写作能力的影响研究[J]. 外语教学, 2020, 41(06):72-76.

张伶俐. "产出导向法"的教学有效性研究[J]. 现代外语, 2017, 40(03):369-376+438.

张素敏, 张继东. "多轮续写"中学习者英语水平的动态发展研究[J]. 外语教学, 2019, 40(06):57-62.

张文娟. "产出导向法"对大学英语写作影响的实验研究[J]. 现代外语, 2017, 40(03):377-385+438-439.

张文忠. 本土化依托项目外语教学的"教学"观[J]. 中国大学教学, 2012(4):47-51.

张文忠. iPBL——本土化的依托项目英语教学模式[J]. 中国外语, 2015, 12(02):15-23.

张秀芹, 张倩. 不同体裁读后续写对协同的影响差异研究[J]. 外语界, 2017(3): 90-96.

张震宇, 洪化清. ChatGPT 支持的外语教学: 赋能、问题与策略[J]. 外语界, 2023(2):38-44.

张征. 多模态 PPT 演示教学与学生学习绩效的相关性研究[J]. 中国外语, 2010, 7(03):54-58.

张征. 多模态 PPT 演示教学与学生学习态度的相关性研究[J]. 外语电化教学, 2013(3):59-64.

Milton Keynes UK
Ingram Content Group UK Ltd.
UKHW031047291124
451807UK00001B/44